Happiness

How to Achieve a Happy Mindset and Live Your Best Life

Lena F. Nooring

© **Copyright 2020 - All rights reserved.**

The content contained within this book may not be reproduced, duplicated or transmitted without direct written permission from the author or the publisher.

Under no circumstances will any blame or legal responsibility be held against the publisher, or author, for any damages, reparation, or monetary loss due to the information contained within this book, either directly or indirectly.

Legal Notice:

This book is copyright protected. It is only for personal use. You cannot amend, distribute, sell, use, quote or paraphrase any part, or the content within this book, without the consent of the author or publisher.

Disclaimer Notice:

Please note the information contained within this document is for educational and entertainment purposes only. All effort has been executed to present accurate, up to date, reliable, complete information. No warranties of any kind are declared or implied. Readers acknowledge that the author is not engaged in the rendering of legal, financial, medical or professional advice. The content within this book has been derived from various sources. Please consult a licensed professional before attempting any techniques outlined in this book.

By reading this document, the reader agrees that under no circumstances is the author responsible for any losses, direct or indirect, that are incurred as a result of the use of the information contained within this document, including, but not limited to, errors, omissions, or inaccuracies.

Table of Contents

INTRODUCTION 1

CHAPTER 1: WHY WE ARE NOT HAPPY 7
- THE IMPORTANCE OF PERCEPTION 19
  - *The Real Reasons We're Unhappy* 31

CHAPTER 2: WHAT IS HAPPINESS? 41
- THE MANY DEFINITIONS OF HAPPINESS 46
  - *True Happiness vs. False Happiness* 51

CHAPTER 3: HAPPINESS STARTS FROM WITHIN 61
- SELF-ACCEPTANCE 63
  - *Cultivating Happy Habits* 67
- GRATITUDE 71
- OPTIMISM 75
- RESILIENCE 79
- KNOWING YOUR VALUES 82

CHAPTER 4: INDULGING YOUR PASSIONS AND INTERESTS ... 85
- FINDING YOUR PASSION 88
  - *Let Your Passions Bring You Happiness* 92
- HOBBIES 95

CHAPTER 5: NO MAN IS AN ISLAND 107
- HAPPINESS IS LOVE 112

CHAPTER 6: SELF-CARE 121
- THE ART OF SELF-LOVE 123

CHAPTER 7: MONEY MATTERS 133
- MONEY VS. HAPPINESS - HOW TO RECONCILE THE TWO 137

CHAPTER 8: THE MEANING OF LIFE **145**
  FINDING YOUR LIFE'S PURPOSE 149
CONCLUSION **155**
REFERENCES **159**

Introduction

Happiness is when what you think, what you say, and what you do are in harmony.

- Mahatma Gandhi

Dissatisfied? Bored? Empty? If any of these words describe you, then you've come to the right place. Happiness is a feeling that too many of us take for granted. Rather than learning how to be happy, we attempt to teach ourselves *not* to be unhappy. Are you feeling dissatisfied? Here's a book on gratitude. Are you feeling bored? Read this article about productivity or finding meaning in the workplace.

Rarely, however, do we actively pursue happiness itself. We see a lot in our popular culture about "practicing" gratitude or "practicing" self-care, but when was the last time someone advised you to "practice" happiness? Yet, happiness, like self-care or gratitude or any other positive cognitive habit, requires practice too. Much like resilience or productivity, happiness is a skill. It's not our natural cognitive state. Learning not to be unhappy is only half the battle.

Think of this book as a practical instruction manual for finding lasting happiness, whatever that means for you. This book will help you to see and seize the opportunities that you know are waiting for you out in the world, the ones that you just can't seem to take for yourself. It will help you to find direction when your life begins to feel stagnant or aimless as well as provide you tangible strategies for letting go of negative or pessimistic thought patterns that may be holding you back in life.

When people are struggling with negative emotions, it's only natural for them to first take steps to manage those negative emotions. If you struggle with anger or depression, then you learn strategies for coping with those feelings. But managing negative emotions doesn't necessarily lead to positive emotions. Learning how to manage your anger doesn't automatically make you feel benevolent or compassionate. The absence of depression isn't happiness.

As such, many people work hard to overcome debilitating negative feelings only to find that their lives almost feel empty or meaningless without them! Without anger or depression or victimhood, who are you? What's your purpose? People find themselves losing joy in activities that once filled them with passion. And others will overcome one negative mood state, like anger, only to have it replaced with another negative mood state, like depression or anxiety. In all of these cases, happiness remains elusive.

If any of this sounds familiar, you can relax. My name is Lena F. Nooring, and I have spent many years now working as a life coach and mentor to at-risk children. I spend 40 hours a week (and often more) helping people to find happiness and meaning within their lives. My philosophy is that it's not enough to manage negative emotions; happiness is something that you have to learn. It's something that you have to actively practice and work toward. It's not the inevitable result of letting go of depression or getting the job of your dreams.

This philosophy is something that I learned the hard way. Before I found my calling, I was trapped for years in a terrible marriage. I believed what many people believe—to be happy, I had to escape my marriage. And finally, I did, traveling all the way across the United States, nearly 3,000 miles, to get away from my toxic relationship and start my life anew.

Leaving my marriage and my hometown was the single best decision I've ever made, without a doubt. But when I arrived in my new city ready to start my life over, I quickly realized something very important: I was still unhappy. Ending my marriage and starting my life over was an improvement, but I didn't have the mental skills to appreciate my new power or freedom. Furthermore, I didn't have the mental skills to create a new life that would fill me with joy. I was still falling prey to old, negative habits and beliefs and finding new reasons in my new life to feel dissatisfied, bored, and angry.

Years later, I have made it my life's mission to learn the art of happiness. Using the skills and strategies that I taught myself so many years ago, I have been able to help hundreds of people learn to live their lives to the fullest. I have been studying life satisfaction for more than five years now and have been working successfully as a life coach for many more. I was able to achieve genuine happiness for myself, but I did it the hard way. With this book as your guide, my hope is to pass on the wisdom and life skills that so dramatically changed the way I viewed the world and helped me to rediscover my love of life.

No matter what rut or mental box you find yourself trapped in, this book has something for you. Over the years, I have developed strategies and techniques for positive life transformation that work for people of all ages, backgrounds, and life experiences. Not every strategy in this book will work for you, but you may be surprised at how effective the simplest techniques can be in transforming your life for the better. Every strategy and suggestion in this book is reinforced with the latest research in psychology and cognitive science as well as the spiritual wisdom from traditions as varied as mindfulness, Buddhism, and stoicism.

This book is essentially divided into two main parts. First, we will learn what happiness is and how to recognize it from a scientific, spiritual, emotional, and practical viewpoint. The first half of this book will explain what happiness looks like in our brains, how it manifests in our lives, and how happiness is a skill rather than an emotion. The second part of the book will teach you how to develop that skill and will be filled with exercises, simple mental techniques, and small practical changes you can make in your daily life to achieve a happiness that is deep, true, and long-lasting. You don't have to move 3,000 miles away from everything you've ever known to find happiness. For most people, happiness is already present in their lives. All they have to do is learn how to see it.

Life is far too short to experience anything but true happiness. Don't allow yourself to live with anything less than that for one more second. If you're ready to take back control of your mind, your feelings, and your life, simply turn the page to get started on your journey.

Chapter 1:

Why We Are Not Happy

Happiness is not something you postpone for the future; it is something you design for the present.

- Jim Rohn

When asked the question "What makes you happy?" most people are quick to answer. Yet, many of the things that we believe make us "happy" are really just serving to mask our inner dissatisfaction with life. Modern technology arguably allows humans to live in far more comfort and luxury than was ever possible in the past, but, though human lives are becoming a little easier, there's no evidence to suggest that human minds are becoming happier. Even if you win the lottery or land the job of your dreams, there are certain mental traps everyone falls prey to that sabotage the ability to find genuine, lasting happiness.

Comparing Yourself With Others

Comparison with myself brings improvement, comparison with others brings discontent.

- Betty Jamie Chung

Everyone's life circumstances are different. Everyone starts at different places in life, and everyone faces different challenges along the way. If you start comparing yourself with others, then you'll always find something wrong with yourself. It's never going to be an even comparison. Rather than fairly comparing yourself against someone else, you'll start weighing their strengths against your weaknesses. And if you are constantly focused on your weaknesses rather than focused on cultivating your strengths, then you can never hope to be anything more than mediocre.

Comparison will put you on the fast-track to dissatisfaction. No matter who you are or what your life is like, there will always be someone out there who has more than you do. There will always be someone smarter, wealthier, more attractive, more qualified. If you spend your time wondering why you aren't more like other people or wishing that you had things that you think other people have, then it becomes difficult to see the goodness and success in your own life.

Rather than comparing yourself unfavorably with others, use their success to inspire you. Stop comparing yourself with others and start comparing yourself with yourself. When you're fully focused on your own fulfillment, you'll start to notice your own strengths, achievements, and accomplishments. Rather than putting yourself down for not being like others, you'll start to celebrate yourself for being who you are. Remember, you are enough.

Lack of Gratitude

What you focus on grows, what you think about expands, and what you dwell upon determines your reality.

- Robin Sharma

Lack of gratitude is one of the most common and pervasive reasons for chronic unhappiness. When we are hyper-focused on the things we don't have, it becomes difficult to see all the things that we do have.

It's easy to see what's missing in life. We all know what we want. What's harder to see is what we already have. Gratitude allows us to look at our lives through a new lens and take a moment to appreciate all the ways we've been lucky, successful, and rewarded. Practicing gratitude isn't about ignoring the bad or difficult things in life; it's simply a way to step back and remind ourselves that it isn't *all* bad. People who don't practice some form of gratitude often find themselves struggling to feel positive, confident, or hopeful about the future.

The momentary joy that we get from physical things doesn't last. And so, when you get that thing you wanted, whether it's a new car or the latest iPhone, it only makes you feel good for a little while. But once the novelty has worn off, you start wanting something else. And while there's nothing wrong with having goals or working toward bigger and better things, it's important to take a step back and remember all of the things you've already acquired.

If we don't take a moment to feel grateful, then we get stuck in an endless loop of wanting more and more and more. Worse, we start to feel like what we have isn't enough. When we don't practice gratitude, we lose our ability to feel satisfied.

When we practice gratitude, one good thing brings us a lifetime of happiness. When we appreciate the things that are in our lives, we start to appreciate life itself. And when we are grateful simply to be here in the world, that is when we start to approach true happiness. Not the momentary rush we get from buying something new or even from achieving a goal. The kind that lasts.

Getting Stuck in Your Comfort Zone

A comfort zone is a really beautiful place, but nothing grows there.

- Anonymous

Hanging out in our comfort zone may feel good in the short term, but in the long term, it prevents us from growing. We get stuck in our comfort zone because it's, well, comfortable. More importantly, it feels safe. And it's very easy to justify staying in a place that feels safe by calling our limiting decisions or beliefs "practical."

Stepping out of your comfort zone doesn't mean putting yourself in any true danger. But it does mean finding the courage within yourself to take the necessary risks you need to take to achieve your dreams.

Every goal comes with a certain level of risk. We can't achieve great things if we aren't willing to do great things. We can't grow or expand if we're too afraid to try new things or learn new skills. Staying in our comfort zone is playing it safe. And while playing it safe is sometimes the practical choice, it can't become a way of life.

If you live your life according to what feels comfortable, then you'll start to miss out on opportunities for transformation. If you start telling yourself that you're "too young" or "too old" to do something you want to do, then you're living in your comfort zone. If you're waiting for the "right" time or the "ideal" moment, then you're living in your comfort zone. These things are just excuses. They're the reasons you're giving yourself to justify *not* pursuing your dreams.

When we mistake comfort for happiness, we often make another, crucial mistake. If comfort equals happiness, then discomfort, we reason, must equal unhappiness. But this is not the case. Being uncomfortable isn't a signal that something is wrong;

it's a signal that something is *different*. Trying something new is always going to feel uncomfortable; it's rare that we pick up a new skill with ease or fit in naturally with a group of strangers. For the majority of our lives, growth requires some level of discomfort. It requires us to do things we're not good at, make mistakes in front of other people, and venture to unknown places without the guidance of experiences to help us. If you're unable to be uncomfortable, you begin to limit yourself and your opportunities to those that lie within your comfort zone. As the name suggests, the comfort zone is where you're comfortable, but it's rarely where you're happy.

Not Moving Your Body Enough

One key way in which modern technology has *not* improved our lives is by eliminating the need to physically move our bodies throughout the day. This is especially true for people whose livelihood or creative passion depends on them sitting in front of a computer screen for eight hours a day. In fact, most American jobs are possible to do in their entirety without the need for you to get up from your desk at all. Not once.

This kind of long-term sedentary lifestyle is extremely detrimental, not only for our physical bodies but for our mental wellness as well. No matter how engaging or intellectually stimulating your work may be, physical exercise plays a key role in the brain's ability to keep you happy. Specifically, exercise causes the brain to release certain chemicals called *endorphins*. These chemicals control a number of things, including dulling your sensitivity to pain. They also trigger positive emotions and are primarily responsible for the way you feel when you say you're "happy." Without some kind of daily exercise, your brain is missing out on these crucial chemicals (Bathla, 2017). In other words, if you don't find a way to move your body every day, you start to become chemically incapable of feeling happiness.

Neglecting the Basics

You can't have the home of your dreams if you struggle to vacuum regularly. You can't become a famous writer if you never write. To put it simply, many of us neglect the basics when pursuing the things that we want. We get frustrated when we can't achieve the things we want to achieve and assume that there's something wrong with us. Maybe we aren't trying hard enough, aren't qualified enough, or aren't smart enough. But have you ever heard the saying "You can't run before you've learned to walk"? You can't start to achieve great things if you're still learning the basics.

It's also important to pay attention to your physical needs. When we think about happiness, we tend to focus on our emotions, thoughts, and moods. But our bodies play a big role in our happiness.

If your body isn't getting the things it needs to function in a healthy way, then it will start to impact your mood. Are you getting enough sleep at night? Are you eating healthy food? You may be surprised by just how much a good night's sleep can change.

Living in the Past or the Future, Never the Present

If you are depressed, you are living in the past. If you are anxious, you are living in the future. If you are at peace, you are living in the present.

- Anonymous

The human mind runs through about 60,000 thoughts every day. More than 95% of these thoughts are repeated (Bathla, 2017). We often get caught up in thoughts, memories, and experiences from the past because these are things that have already happened to us. We don't question or scrutinize our past-related thoughts because the past is what makes up our experiences and, therefore, plays a huge role in shaping our identities.

And when we're not in the past, we seem to find ourselves stuck in the future. We are constantly anxious about the things that might be coming around the corner. And somehow, it seems to be much easier to imagine a future that's dark and dangerous over one in which everything works out okay.

Whether you're focused on the past or the future, you're not focused on the present moment. You can't take any real action to change your life because you aren't living in the here and now.

Many of the feelings, fears, beliefs, and assumptions we carry around with us on a daily basis are not rooted in reality; they come from things that happened to us in the past or things that we imagine will happen to us in the future. To some degree, it's perfectly healthy and advisable to rely on past experience or to plan for the future. But if you spend all your time living in the past, then you stop reacting to the situations that are right in front of you, and you get stuck repeating the patterns of the past. Just because something happened before doesn't mean it will happen again. Just because you had certain habits, attitudes, or beliefs in the past doesn't mean you have to have those things now.

Similarly, we are limited when we are constantly looking to the future. No plans are perfect; it's quite rare that things unfold according to our expectations. If you fall apart every time life deviates from your plans, then it will be difficult for you to seize new opportunities or let go of limiting beliefs.

The more stuck you get in the past or the future, the further removed you become from reality. And the more removed you become from reality, the more powerless you feel to change it. But the reality is that the present is the only thing that you *can* change. You can't go back and change things that happened in the past. You can't jump forward in time to see the future. And if you prevent yourself from participating fully in your present, then you will start to feel truly stuck.

To alleviate yourself from the unpleasantness of anxiety, you must learn to let go of the past and the future and pay attention to what's right in front of you. The more actively you start to participate in your own life, the more power you will have to bring good things your way.

You May Be More Than Sad

Often, all it takes to bring more happiness into your life are a few simple changes to your daily habits. But depression, on the other hand, is going to take much more than that. Sadness is an emotion, one that comes and goes in response to negative thoughts and life circumstances. But depression is a major mood disorder, one that can completely change the way you think and keep you trapped in extremely dark moments of despair and hopelessness.

Letting go of the toxic habits in this chapter will certainly help you to manage depression. But if you feel like your negative feelings are more than sadness, it's important to reach out to a mental health professional who can give you the guidance you need to manage your depression in an effective and healthy way.

Spending Too Much Time on Social Media

Social media isn't all bad. In many ways, it's enabled us to become more connected as a global society. However, too much time on social media can have some extremely negative consequences, especially when it comes to our mood and our cognitive abilities.

Too much time on social media has been linked to all kinds of nasty side effects, including increased anxiety, depression, and dissatisfaction, as well as a decreased ability to focus, connect with others in real life, and remember things. The fact of the matter is social media makes it too easy for us to compare ourselves to others. Even if you know that people typically put their best foot forward on social media, it's hard to keep that in mind when you're scrolling through picture after picture of everyone else's idealized lives. Increased advertising on major social media platforms also makes it easy to feel like we don't have enough in our lives. When you're constantly getting advertisements persuading you to buy something new, it becomes more difficult to appreciate what you already have.

Putting Too Much Stock in Material Things

Beautiful clothes, nice furniture, the latest technological gadgets—all these and more make our lives more pleasant, more comfortable, and sometimes more successful. Material things *can* bring us happiness. Think of a thoughtful gift from a partner, a home-cooked meal, a Christmas card from a child. But too many of us have become over-reliant on material things for happiness and comfort, so we stop seeking it from other places.

Our culture is a materialistic one. Most American jobs involve selling something, whether it be material goods, digital products, or services. The internet is flooded with advertisements, all of which are encouraging us to buy something new, sign up for a new app, or purchase a new service. Our livelihood, our social interactions, and our culture-at-large are based around the buying and selling of material goods, and this has caused a deep dysfunction when it comes to finding happiness. Too many of us turn to material things for happiness when what we really need may be something that money can't buy, like a hug from a loved one or feedback from a supervisor.

When we cling to material things for happiness and comfort, we also tend to give a lot less than we get. If we believe that material things are the road to happiness, then we aren't going to want to give up anything that we've managed to acquire. But the reality is that giving to others is one of the major roads to happiness because the more focused you are on yourself, the more miserable you start to become.

Being Surrounded by Negativity

No matter how much work you do to let go of limiting cognitive habits, happiness isn't only about you. If you're surrounded by negative people, then you'll start to pick up their negative habits and worldviews. If your coworkers constantly complain, it will become more difficult for you to feel satisfied with your work. If your family members are constantly putting each other down, then it will become more difficult for you to see their good qualities. We can't always pick and choose the people in our social circle. But limiting your exposure to negative people as much as possible can go a surprisingly long way in lifting your mood or improving your outlook on life.

The Importance of Perception

All of these cognitive or social habits are things that can slowly but surely eat away at our happiness. And these things aren't just the habits of the unhappy few. Due to a number of social and cultural factors, these toxic habits are ones that almost all of us struggle with on a daily basis.

But to truly find happiness, we can't just change our habits; we have to change our perceptions. The lens through which we look at the world is what will either help or prevent us from achieving true satisfaction. There are certain common perceptions that prevent us from seeing the world in a positive light.

Seeing Yourself as a Victim

Having a victim mentality is one of the most destructive views you can have of the world. When you start to see yourself as a victim, you start to see yourself as powerless. If you believe everything bad that happens in your life has been done *to* you, then you lose your ability to find lasting solutions to your problems. If you see yourself as a victim, then your feelings, actions, and successes all become dependent on the goodwill of other people. Worse, the more you internalize your victimhood, the more difficult it will be to take back control of your own life. If being a victim is part of your identity, then empowering yourself will cause you to question who you are as a person, and that can be scary for a lot of people.

A victim mentality is connected to the toxic mental habit of comparing oneself to others. The reality is that every human's life is different. Everyone is born into slightly different circumstances and will travel their own unique journey toward success. The habit of comparing yourself with others will put you in a constant state of discontent, and that constant state of discontent can quickly morph into the perception of yourself as a perpetual victim. Comparing the strengths of others against your weaknesses can only serve to make you feel powerless. People who focus on their strengths tend to continuously improve themselves. But people who focus on their weaknesses struggle to move beyond mediocre (Bathla, 2020).

If you're constantly asking "Why me?" or "Why not me?" then you become paralyzed by your misfortunes or failures. But if you look at other people's successes as inspiration, then you can start to take action to change your situation. Comparing yourself with others can easily cause you to believe that nothing good ever happens to you or even that other people are actively working to harm you. But if you can learn to compare yourself with yourself, then you can start to let go of your victim mentality and start taking responsibility for your own life. Victim mentalities are rooted in a lack of fulfillment. And fulfillment only comes when you've given everything your best shot. If you believe that you are enough, then you can let go of the belief that other people are responsible for your happiness.

The Need to Impress

The constant need to impress others also comes from a shift in mental focus. When we are secure in ourselves and believe in our own inherent worth, then we don't need validation from other people to feel proud, confident, or worthy. But when we are insecure, we start to doubt ourselves. Deep inside, we believe that we aren't good enough, that we somehow aren't worthy of other people's love or respect. As such, we start to spend a great deal of time and energy seeking approval from other people rather than pursuing the things that bring us genuine happiness or satisfaction.

Getting vs. Giving

If your entire mental focus is on getting what you need or want, then you stop pursuing one of life's fundamental joys: giving. If you believe you don't have enough money, then you will be less likely to give to those who could use a boost. If you believe you don't have enough time, then you will stop valuing the time you have with loved ones.

Ironically, if we feel there's a lack of something in our lives, our pursuit of that missing thing causes us to have less of it. The more money we want, the less we seem to have. The more time we want, the less we appreciate what we have. And the more energy we want, the more tired we seem to feel.

Cynicism

Awe is an emotion that, unfortunately, our culture has come to view as childlike. People who are openly amazed, intrigued, or impressed are sometimes viewed as naive or uninformed. But this is not the case. Simply put, the world is amazing. Admitting that other people are impressive or that other places are interesting should never reflect badly on yourself. People who are unable to feel (or admit to feeling) awe are often deeply insecure. The desire to never appear impressed or interested in anything comes from a deep distrust of human emotions, especially our own. Too many of us are taught to fear our feelings as children, and so we cut ourselves off from our emotions as adults. But the ability to feel and express our emotions is critical to our health and wellness.

Isolation

Feeling socially or emotionally distant from other people is also rooted in perception. Isolation and loneliness come from the deep-seated belief that we are fundamentally different from other people. When we are in social situations, we feel confused, agitated, anxious, or otherwise uncomfortable because we are insecure. We are so focused on how we differ from other people that we don't notice how we are alike. We become so invested in the things we said or did that were "wrong" that we fail to notice when we say something witty or clever or interesting. Isolation is often rooted in the need to be socially validated by other people. We believe that when others disagree with us, it's because we did something wrong. We believe that if others aren't reaching out to us, it's because they don't want to be with us. But these beliefs are rooted in insecurity, not reality.

Failure to Set Goals

The failure to set goals is also the result of certain beliefs about ourselves. In this case, it's the belief that we aren't responsible for our own happiness or success. Those who believe that they have the power to change their own lives will naturally begin to turn their dreams into achievable goals. But those who don't often get stuck dreaming. Rather than taking steps to make their dreams come true, they simply drift through life, waiting for their dreams to happen to them. People who don't feel empowered tend to say to themselves "I wish that X would happen," while people who do feel empowered tend to say to themselves "How can I make X happen?"

Erroneous Ideas About Happiness

Our ideas about what happiness is (or isn't) can often prevent us from achieving it. For example, consider a recent study that measured the happiness levels in people who won the lottery versus people who became paralyzed from the waist down. As you might expect, the study found that in the first year after the defining incident, lottery winners were significantly happier than paraplegics. But after the first year, the study found that people's happiness levels began to revert to the levels they experienced before the defining event. Paraplegics began to find joy and happiness again as they adjusted to their new situation and moved on with their lives. Lottery winners, on the other hand, also adjusted to their new levels of wealth and financial security. And once they did, they became just as vulnerable to toxic habits and perceptions as they had been before they won (Pomeroy, 2014).

To achieve lasting happiness, there are some common happiness myths that we need to let go of:

1. *Happiness is instant.*

Lasting happiness doesn't happen overnight. Healing, growing, and ridding yourself of your problems are all long-term processes. If you wait for big, dramatic changes to feel happy, then you're going to spend a lot of time feeling miserable.

More to the point, our brains are physically incapable of feeling happiness for an extended period. Instead, we are equipped with "hedonic set points" that establish our base mood (optimistic, pessimistic, or indifferent). These set points also adapt very quickly to our surroundings. This is why winning the lottery can't permanently make us happy, just as becoming paralyzed can't make us permanently miserable (Dee, 2011).

2. *Happiness is external.*

Often, we look to external things, like money or relationships or career success, to make us happy. But external things can only bring us short-term happiness because external things are impermanent. If you rely on a career or a relationship to make you happy, then you will be unable to maintain happiness if that job ends or that relationship becomes tense (Cherry, 2020). Happiness isn't something that happens to you; it's a choice, something that you actively decide to cultivate.

In fact, there's evidence to suggest acquiring more material things can make you *un*happy. If you're constantly focused on acquiring more, then it becomes difficult for you to feel satisfied with the things you already have. New purchases can also come with new worries, whether those take the form of repairs, extra maintenance, or simply the financial burden of the purchase. Instead, there's a great deal of research to suggest that investing your money in new or fun experiences is far more satisfying than spending it on material objects (Becker, 2020).

Money is another external source that many people believe will make them happy. And while it's true that having enough money to meet your basic needs can certainly improve your quality of life, there's no evidence to suggest that an excess of wealth will make you any more content with your life (Wolff, 2018).

Alongside fortune, many of us believe fame is the secret to happiness. But once achieved, fame can be a trap, causing people to feel like they have to live up to certain expectations or social perceptions to maintain their very public image. This continuous lack of privacy can be extremely draining and difficult in the long run. Relying on fame for happiness inextricably ties the achievement of your life goals to the approval of others, which inherently prevents them from having any lasting meaning (Jones, 2009).

Many people blame their unhappiness on the place that they live. But while big cities like Berlin or Dubai may seem glamorous, there's research to suggest that happiness decreases as population density increases. Glamorous cities also tend to come with a much higher cost of living, which can lower one's quality of life and, therefore, be a cause of unhappiness.

We also tend to place a great deal of happiness expectations on our romantic partners. Inevitably, the partner of our dreams tends to have movie-star looks, but these have nothing to do with how loving or caring a person can be. In fact, there's research to suggest that most people end up with mates that are about equally attractive to themselves. And a recent study found that having lots of sex isn't the answer either. Increased sexual activity did not necessarily result in an increase in happiness in a romantic partnership.

Even if you do have a relationship, that's not guaranteed to bring you happiness, either. Truly happy relationships often require a great deal of hard work to achieve and maintain. And if your happiness is dependent on your partner, then you will find yourself unable to be happy in their absence or worse, if you do things that make you unhappy just to please your partner (Tan, 2017).

A good-looking partner doesn't bring happiness, and neither does being good-looking ourselves. Studies have found that people who are more universally considered "attractive" are just as likely to experience self-esteem issues as those who aren't. In fact, attractive people find it more difficult to accept compliments, not only about their looks but about their success in other areas of life as well.

Long or extravagant vacations are another external pin on which many people place their hopes of happiness. But there are studies that suggest a two-week vacation is not inherently more satisfying or restful than a one-week one. The difference doesn't lie in how much time you have but how you spend that time.

Freedom is another concept that many of us tend to equate with happiness, but having too many choices has been found to make people less happy, not more. The more difficult our selection process is, the more anxiety we have, and the less satisfaction we feel when we make a good decision (Dee, 2011).

3. *Happiness is a destination.*

Have you ever caught yourself saying something along the lines of "I'll be happy when…"? Many of us believe that happiness has a finish line, and once we cross it, then we'll never feel unhappy again. So many of us move through life believing that if we can just reach a certain place, then we'll be blessed with a permanent sense of contentment. Once you reach your happiness destination, everything will be easy forever after.

This, however, is not reality. Happiness isn't a destination; it's a mindset. Yes, happiness is something that we must work toward, but there's no final destination. There is no point of permanent happiness. Instead, it's something that we must continue to practice throughout our lifetime (Orsini, 2019).

4. *Happiness is the goal.*

Happiness is a mercurial concept. It's something that not only changes from person to person but has also changed throughout history. The ancient Greeks, for example, believed that happiness was the result of pure luck. Either the gods blessed you or they didn't. In the meantime, all you could do was your best with what you had. Happiness wasn't something to work toward; it was something to appreciate if and when it did appear.

Medieval Europe believed that happiness was only something your soul achieved in heaven after you died. And during the Renaissance, another happiness myth was born, the idea that happiness is simply the presence of pleasure. For them, however, "pleasure" typically meant achieving success. But today, we take this more literally, mistakenly believing that happiness can be found in physical comforts or conveniences.

During the Enlightenment, happiness was considered a basic human right, something that all people deserved to have. And while we still have this belief, we're not quite sure what that basic right entails. Worse, it has led us to believe that we are somehow entitled to a "happily ever after." It's similar to the myth that working hard will lead to success. Yes, practicing happiness will improve your general satisfaction with life, but it's not an inevitable or automatic reward that comes from achieving your goals or having good things happen to you (Dee, 2011).

5. *Happiness is the absence of pain.*

In all cultures, Hell is depicted as a place of pain and suffering, and it makes sense. How can we possibly feel happy if we're in pain? But take a lesson from the paraplegics in the happiness study. Pain can cause us distress at first, but in the long run, it can also make us stronger, wiser, and more resilient to future suffering, qualities that paradoxically lead us closer to happiness (Vozza, 2018).

6. *Happiness is success.*

Success does bring happiness, but only in the short term. One of the biggest mistakes we make as a society is believing that success is related to long-term happiness. But often, we measure success based on material or social accomplishments, like making a lot of money or having a happy romantic relationship. Attaining these things is like winning the lottery. They make you happy at first, but then you adjust to your new reality. Happiness is not success, but success is happiness; the more happiness you have in your life, the more good things seem to come your way (Tan, 2017).

7. *Happiness is the presence of pleasure.*

When asked, many people would agree that happiness is the same as feeling good. Just as we equate Hell with constant suffering, most of us imagine Heaven as a place where we feel good all the time. However, if feeling good were our only requirement, then doing drugs or having sex every day would be enough to make us happy, right? And most of us can agree that's not the case. At the end of the day, feeling good doesn't lead to lasting happiness because our moods don't give our lives meaning. Often, it's things that sometimes make our lives difficult, like our jobs or relationships, that also bring us the most joy (Parks, 2021).

8. *Happiness is achieving your dreams.*

Landing your dream job or achieving your life's goal may seem like a long-term ticket to happiness, but it's the same as winning the lottery. Immediately after the accomplishment, you will feel a surge of well-being. Your life will drastically change for the better, and you will feel secure in the knowledge that you're living the life you've always wanted to live.

But then you'll adjust to your new reality. If you're making more money, then your lifestyle will slowly but surely begin to match your new budget. You may start to dislike your coworkers or get a new boss that you don't like as much. Gradually, your dream job will become just your job, and you'll find yourself with new dreams, new goals, and new ambitions. This may sound dark, but this is perfectly healthy and normal. Life is always changing, and if it wasn't, then we would become bored and discontent. Lasting happiness is found not in our achievements but in the *pursuit* of our goals (Lyubomirsky, n.d.)

The Real Reasons We're Unhappy

We all know when we aren't happy, but our toxic habits and perceptions can lead us astray when it comes to finding the true cause of our unhappiness. Sadness and depression are usually triggered by challenging life experiences. But often, those challenges aren't so obvious, making it difficult for us to make lasting or effective changes. The toxic mental habits and perceptions listed in this chapter are toxic because they are all major triggers for sadness and depression. All of these habits and perceptions are the result of chronic surface-level thinking. We spend too much time looking for external causes of unhappiness and not enough time looking within ourselves. There are a few in particular that can really make it challenging for us to find lasting happiness in our lives (Brolley, 2019).

Meaninglessness

According to Bertrand Russell, a 1930s philosopher, one of the eight major causes of unhappiness is what he called "meaninglessness." Pervasive pessimism, he felt, created a kind of cultural depression. People who over-identified with feelings of cynicism and negativity simply didn't allow themselves to feel positive emotions like joy, wonder, or hope. Over time, preventing yourself from feeling positive feelings prevents you from feeling any feelings at all, a mental state that inevitably ends in depression. Allowing yourself to feel strong emotions means allowing yourself to care about yourself, other people, the fate of the world, etc. If you don't care about anything, then it's impossible for you to feel any kind of lasting contentment or happiness (Tim, 2018).

Over-Identification With Your Emotions

That being said, being controlled or overwhelmed by your emotions can also lead to unhappiness. Allowing negative emotions to completely derail your life will inevitably prevent you from finding lasting positivity. It's one thing to fully experience negative emotions, but it's altogether different to let them control your actions or sabotage your successes. Emotions are simply responses to events happening around and sometimes within us. Over-identifying with those responses can prevent you from having a realistic view of yourself. Worse, giving in to strong emotions can cause you to give up responsibility for your own life. Daily habits like journaling or exercising can help you to cultivate a balanced relationship with your emotions by providing them a healthy outlet.

Surrounding Yourself With Negativity

Even if you don't actively participate, surrounding yourself with negative people will inevitably erode your ability to remain positive. Of course, this doesn't mean that you should cut off your loved ones at the first sign of unhappiness. But it does mean that you should take steps to distance yourself from people with an established pattern of negative behavior.

Anyone who makes you feel worthless or anxious is not someone you should be investing a great deal of time in. Not only are they engendering negative feelings within you, but they are also preventing you from feeling positive emotions like pride or security. Instead, try spending more time with people who inspire you or make you want to be the best version of yourself.

That being said, we can't always control who we spend our time with. It's not always healthy to cut yourself off from a coworker or family member. In situations like this, it's important to learn how to lay good boundaries. An easy way to change the course of a negative conversation is by asking the other person how they intend to fix the problems they are complaining about. This will either end the conversation or transform it into something more positive and productive (Bradberry, 2016).

Judgment

In many ways, it's healthy and even advisable to hold yourself to high standards. But if you set yourself goals that are too lofty, you're setting yourself up for disappointment. The same is true for other people. If you hold others to impossibly high standards, then you're inevitably going to be angry and disappointed when others fail to meet them. Judgment and criticism, whether they are directed at ourselves or others, prevent us from feeling love or happiness. Often, the things that we are most judgmental of in others are reflections of things that we fear or are insecure about in ourselves.

This brings us to another of Bertrand Russell's causes of unhappiness, competition. He believed, as we all do, that competition inspires us to succeed, but only by comparing ourselves against another person's failures. If we're constantly in a battle with other people to get ahead, then our successes are ultimately meaningless. We didn't achieve them for the sake of our own improvement; we achieved them for the sake of being better than others. And there's always going to be someone out there who's "better" than you. If you view life through the lens of "winners" and "losers," then you're always going to see yourself as a loser because there's always going to be someone out there who challenges your sense of self-worth.

Judgment and criticism are also related to the seventh of Bertrand Russell's causes of unhappiness, what he called "persecution mania." This is what happens when we start to lash out at other people for not doing enough for us. We start to blame our negative feelings or failures on others ("He never appreciates anything I do for him!" or "People at work are constantly spreading rumors about me!") rather than taking action to change our situation. Not only can this deeply damage our interpersonal relationships, but it can lead to a victim mentality, keeping us trapped in the negative belief that other people are out to get us.

Failure to Set Goals

A failure to set goals is rooted in the third and fourth of Bertrand Russell's causes of unhappiness, boredom and fatigue. When we become too complacent in our lives, we start to feel dissatisfied. A certain level of challenge and stimulation is necessary for us to feel like our lives have purpose and meaning. To set realistic goals for yourself, you have to be willing to challenge yourself. Though the challenge may seem scary, it's necessary to keep you feeling engaged in your life.

On the flip side, if you've set yourself goals that are too high or too vague, then you start to experience what Bertrand Russell called "fatigue," but what we in the modern age typically call "burn out." If you're trying to do too much all at once, then you ultimately won't achieve anything at all. It's great to feel stimulated and productive, but you also have to give yourself a break every once in a while. Holding yourself to insanely high standards can be motivating, but it will ultimately prevent you from achieving lasting success.

A failure to set goals can also lead to the sixth of Bertrand Russell's causes of unhappiness, guilt or shame. Guilt is what we feel when we let ourselves or others down. More often than not, this happens when we fail to give something our best shot. Guilt arises when we fail because of what we *didn't* do, not because of what we *did* do. Failure to set goals can often come from deep-seated feelings of shame and inadequacy. We fail to push or challenge ourselves to succeed because, deep inside, we don't believe we really have the power to achieve our dreams.

Materialism

Have you ever heard the expression "Money can't buy happiness"? Materialism is an over-reliance on material goods and services to make ourselves happy. This doesn't mean, however, that material things have *no* impact on or relevance to our happiness. In fact, a recent study found that money can have a positive impact on your mood, but only if you use it to buy experiences or spend it on other people (Brolley, 2019).

One of our biggest and most toxic cultural myths is that wealth and fame bring happiness. But materialism is rooted in a crucial misunderstanding between comfort and happiness. Buying a car or owning your own home may make your life easier, but these things won't necessarily make you happier (Wolff, 2018).

Materialism often triggers the fifth of Bertrand Russell's causes of unhappiness: envy. The constant pursuit of material wealth inevitably causes us to compare ourselves with others. We see a new car appear in the neighbor's driveway or pictures of a friend's vacation on social media, and suddenly, we are overwhelmed with feelings of inadequacy. We find ourselves wanting those things too, not because they're things that will bring us genuine happiness but because they're things that we don't have.

Social Media

According to a 2019 survey, the average person spends two hours and twenty-two minutes a day on social media. This might not seem like a lot of time, but for all its benefits, social media exposure can lead to some bad mental habits and, subsequently, to negative mood states like depression. You don't have to give up social media entirely to be happy, but it's important to develop a healthy relationship with it (Brolley, 2019).

A recent study by the Happiness Research Institute was conducted to determine just how much social media exposure can influence our mood. In the study, half of the participants were instructed to use Facebook as they normally would, while the other half were instructed not to use Facebook at all for an entire week. At the end of the study, the people who abstained from Facebook use reported feeling much happier and less sad than the Facebook users. They also reported much higher feelings of satisfaction and lower feelings of loneliness. The Facebook users, on the other hand, were 55% more likely to feel stressed. Furthermore, reducing the daily Facebook time by just 20 minutes led to an 18% increase in participants' ability to feel present in the moment. And as you know, being disconnected from the present moment is a major trigger for sadness and depression (Brolley, 2019).

Social media traps us in the eighth and final reason Bertrand Russell gives for unhappiness, fear of public opinion. Social media asks us to make our lives extremely public and often makes us feel afraid to be ourselves. Fear of criticism or negative reactions to our content can cause us to live in constant fear of doing something "wrong" and prevent us from taking risks or fully accepting ourselves for who we really are.

Relying on False Happiness

There's a big difference between a fleeting moment of pleasure and a sense of inner happiness that remains constant regardless of external events. Real happiness comes with a sense of peace, while false happiness is often accompanied by insecurities and doubts. False happiness is often followed by a sense of superiority, but real happiness is about taking joy in other people's successes, not just our own. Furthermore, praise or approval from others can only lead to fleeting happiness because lasting happiness comes from our self-esteem. Confidence and pride in oneself aren't things that others can give you; these are things you have to cultivate within yourself.

This is why happiness ultimately can't be tied to your successes or achievements. No success is permanent. Eventually, inevitably, we will move on to bigger and better goals. True happiness is related to self-transcendence, the ongoing process of personal growth and self-improvement. Ultimately, we find lasting happiness in the process of striving for a better life, not in the achievement of obtaining it.

When we engage in toxic habits and perceptions, we are living only for ourselves. But true, abiding happiness asks us to live in community and harmony with others.

You can't find lasting happiness if you're consumed with your own needs and ambitions because you can't find lasting happiness without meaningful connections with others (Tejvan, 2008).

Now that we know what habits and perceptions prevent us from finding true happiness, it's time to take a closer look at what true happiness really means.

Chapter 2:

What Is Happiness?

Though happiness has been a human pursuit for as long as we've been a species, happiness research is relatively new to the fields of psychology and cognitive science. Happiness research focuses its studies on what happiness is and how to experience it. Since the foundation of psychology in the mid-19th century, the discipline has been mostly focused on what is problematic or disordered in human lives. The medical model developed in the 20th century was focused on diagnosing disorders, neurosis, and pathologies and paid little attention to people who seemed relatively happy or healthy. As such, the vast majority of psychological funding and research over the past 100 years has been poured into the people who have struggled the most to be happy in life, such as people with severe mental illnesses or disorders. And while there's certainly nothing wrong with this, recent years have seen a shift in focus from exclusively helping those with more severe problems to helping all people achieve a higher level of overall happiness (Nelson-Coffey, 2020).

Positive psychology is a new branch of psychology that is focused on the opposite of severe mental illness.

Instead, happiness research is focused on how thoughts, actions, and behaviors make human beings feel true, lasting happiness. This new science has led to a number of discoveries that are radically changing the way we understand happiness and its pursuit.

As we learn more about what happiness is and what drives it, a number of different definitions of happiness have appeared in the last few years. In general, however, researchers define happiness as the positive emotions we feel in response to pleasurable activities. It's a mood state characterized by contentment and general satisfaction with one's life. In essence, happiness is comprised of two basic components:

- Life satisfaction - How fulfilled or content you are with your life, such as finding meaning in your work or feeling close to your family, and
- Balance of emotions - Experiencing a relatively balanced range of emotions on a daily basis with normal ups and downs.

Happiness is nourished by positive emotions, such as pleasure, comfort, or gratitude. Psychologists sometimes refer to happiness in studies as "hedonia," or the presence of positive emotions and the absence of negative ones (Nelson-Coffey, 2020).

"Symptoms" of happiness include:

- The feeling that you are living the life you want to live

- The feeling that the conditions that define your life are good overall
- The feeling that you have accomplished, or have the ability to accomplish, the things you want in life
- An overall feeling of satisfaction with your life
- In general, feeling more positive than negative

In positive psychology, "happiness" is sometimes referred to by its clinical term subjective well-being or SWB. And while there are a number of different scientific theories about what happiness is and what causes it, there are a few commonalities:

- Happiness is a good thing and something that people enjoy feeling.
- Happiness can be either a momentary, fleeting emotion or a long-term mental state.
- A certain percentage of happiness is genetic, though scientists debate just how much of our ability to be happy is biological.
- Pleasure and happiness are two distinct experiences; one does not necessarily lead to the other.

Researchers also agree that happiness rarely comes from one key source. Rather, it is made up of a number of different components. These components all work together in any given moment to contribute (or detract) from our overall happiness. These components include (Nelson-Coffey, 2020):

- Personality
- Emotions (positive and/or negative)
- Physical health
- Social status and/or wealth
- Attachment and relatedness
- Goals and self-efficacy
- Time and place

Very recent research suggests that performing acts of kindness, however, can override many of these factors and have a powerful impact on our feelings of happiness and well-being regardless of the realities of our situation. More studies have come to some shocking conclusions that challenge ideas that we have taken for granted about happiness as a society, such as (Nelson-Coffey, 2020):

- Trying too hard to be happy can often result in selfishness.
- Pursuing happiness through social connections is the most effective method of achieving true happiness.
- Vague happiness goals are easier to obtain than specific ones.
- Happiness makes us better citizens and is the number one predictor of positive civic engagement.

- Happiness is indirectly correlated with religious or spiritual practice. Overall, those with strong religious or spiritual beliefs have been found to show higher levels of compassion toward others. The more compassion one has, the more likely one is to show emotional support to others. And showing emotional support to others is directly correlated with happiness.

Another thing that researchers have found to be directly correlated with happiness is workplace productivity. There has been an explosion of research in recent years about happiness in the workplace, mostly funded by companies seeking to strengthen happiness at work, improve productivity, and attract new talent. Though it may seem obvious that happy employees make a better workspace, up until very recently, it was a common belief that happy employees would be lazy and unproductive workers. However, not only have recent studies found that to be simply untrue, but they have also come to a number of other surprising conclusions, including (Nelson-Coffey, 2020):

- Happy employees are more likely to engage in behaviors that bring more happiness into the workplace for coworkers, management, and customers alike.
- Happiness is directly correlated with improved job performance.

- Unit and/or team happiness is directly correlated with a number of positive outcomes, including higher customer satisfaction and increased company profits.
- General happiness across an organization is directly correlated to increased productivity and company success.

In other words, happiness researchers are finding that individual, team, and company-wide happiness levels have a direct and measurable effect on business success. While there are still a number of questions that remain to be answered, it's clear to researchers that there is a definitive link between happiness and productivity.

The Many Definitions of Happiness

Though everyone experiences happiness, each person has a slightly different perception of what that word means. And there does not seem to be one universal sensation, experience, or event that makes all people happy. But what is clear is that the presence or absence of true happiness can have a huge impact on the way a person experiences their life. Happiness has a big impact on the decisions we make, the way we relate to others, and the quality of our daily existence. So while researchers have yet to pin down a universal definition of happiness, what studies have been done offer us valuable insight into this ever-important emotion.

Applying the scientific method to the study of happiness allows us to see this emotion in ways we've never seen it before. Past generations have left the pursuit of happiness to religion, the arts, and politics. But science can offer us insight into the way happiness appears in our brains, our genetics, and our species. And science can give us insights that transcend culture, social norms, or political realities.

But science is not the first human discipline that has sought to define happiness. The *Oxford English Dictionary* defines happiness as "the state of being happy." Not exactly helpful or illuminating. But the same dictionary offers more clarity under the entry for the word "happy." The *OED* defines "happy" as "feeling or showing pleasure or contentment."

Linguistically speaking, then, happiness is related to feelings of pleasure or contentment. It's the state we're in when we are experiencing or showing those feelings to others. But there's even more information that we can gain from this deceptively simple definition:

- Happiness is a "state," not an emotion or a personality trait. It's not as fleeting as an emotion, but it's not an inherent part of who we are.
- Happiness is equated with mild feelings like pleasure and contentment, distinguishing it

from more intense emotions like joy, ecstasy, or bliss. When looking for happiness, then, we can expect it to be something relatively subtle.
- Happiness can be both an internal (feeling) or external (showing) experience. It can be something that we experience within ourselves, and it can also be something that we share with others.

In most languages around the world, the word "happy" is etymologically linked with the word for "luck." This is especially true of Indo-European languages. For example, the Old French word "heur" gives us the modern French "bonheur," which means both luck and happiness. The German word "gluck" also means both luck and happiness. This linguistic link suggests that humans in the ancient world equated happiness with good fortune more than anything else. In other words, while people today tend to see happiness as a crucial factor in living a full life, ancient people may have seen happiness as a kind of bonus, something over and above the pursuit of a full life (Ackerman, 2020).

But our contemporary definition of "happiness" seems to be a little more complex. In 2019, a Google search of the word "happiness" turned up over two million results. Typing the same work into PsycINFO, one of psychology's most comprehensive databases, will turn up over 19,000 results across a number of academic and popular journals (Ackerman, 2020).

The reason for this many results is that there is still no cohesive, scientific agreement as to what happiness is exactly. According to one group of researchers, there are three main ways that happiness can be approached from a scientific viewpoint (Ackerman, 2020):

- As a global assessment of life and all its many factors
- As a recollection of past emotional experiences
- As a collection of many emotional experiences throughout an individual's lifetime

To further complicate matters, while we all can agree on what happiness feels like, it's much more difficult to find ways to measure happiness. But the general agreement is that happiness is a mental state that features feelings of contentment and satisfaction with one's life.

The *Oxford English Dictionary* describes happiness as the state of feeling pleasure. So what, then, is the difference between pleasure and happiness? Though the two words are often used interchangeably, positive psychology tells us there is a distinct difference between the two. Happiness, as we know, is a state of contentment and general satisfaction. Pleasure, on the other hand, is a visceral, momentary experience. Pleasure is a sensory-based feeling, one that we might get from eating delicious food or getting a massage. Happiness, while transient, is a more long-lasting and stable feeling than pleasure. Happiness tends to last at least a few moments, while pleasure can come and go within seconds.

Pleasure, then, can contribute to happiness, and happiness can enhance feelings of pleasure, but the two are not interchangeable from a psychological perspective. You can derive happiness from a sense of purpose or engagement that isn't pleasurable, and you can simultaneously feel pleasure and unhappiness.

There's a lot of advice out there that encourages us to find meaning in our lives. If we can find meaning or purpose, many claim, then we can find happiness too. And while it's true that meaning and happiness are related to each other, the relationship isn't as close as we might think.

For one thing, meaning is far more stable and long-lasting than happiness. As such, the ways that we maintain or pursue meaning in our lives can be very different from the way we maintain or pursue happiness. A 2016 study found some small but important differences between the way that we experience happiness and meaning (Ackerman, 2020):

- The perception of life as "easy" or "difficult" is correlated with happiness but not meaning.
- Feelings of physical and/or mental health are correlated with happiness but not meaning.
- Feeling good is correlated with feelings of happiness, not meaning.

- Financial hardship reduces feelings of happiness significantly more than it reduces feelings of purpose.
- People with more meaningful lives are more likely to believe that relationships are more important than achievements.
- A likelihood to help others is correlated with meaning, not happiness.
- Happiness is more closely correlated with taking or receiving than giving, while meaning is more closely correlated with giving than with taking or receiving.
- The more people feel that their daily activities are aligned with their core values, the more meaningful they feel their lives to be.

All of these studies have shown that, while meaning and happiness are linked, they are also very different experiences.

True Happiness vs. False Happiness

Rather than defining happiness in terms of "true" or "false," I like to make the distinction between "short-term" and "long-term" happiness.

When people talk about happiness, they can be referring to how they feel in the moment or how they feel about their life in general. Short-term happiness comes from things that make us feel good in the moment but fail to bring us a deeper, more stable sense of contentment. Doing drugs, for example, might make you feel good in the moment, but they can cause a great deal of misery and suffering in your life overall. Pleasure can contribute to feelings of happiness, but the happiness that pleasure brings is also fleeting. Furthermore, the pursuit of pleasure seems to put people at odds with another life course that is crucial to happiness—the pursuit of meaning.

"True" or long-lasting happiness, then, seems to lie at the crossroads between pleasure and meaning, between feeling good and feeling accomplished. It is not a constant state of pleasure or euphoria. The experience of true happiness includes the experience of negative emotions. In other words, happy people can still feel negative emotions like anger or frustration. But happy people have an underlying sense of resilience, a core optimism that helps them to let go of these negative feelings.

Like drugs or pleasure, money is something that only brings us momentary happiness. Beyond a certain point, it cannot give us happiness that is deeper or more long-lasting. This is why no raise ever seems to be enough, no promotion ever high enough. No matter what heights you achieve, you could always have more. The pursuit of higher and ever loftier goals may bring us a sense of purpose, but it certainly doesn't bring us a sense of lasting happiness.

Understanding what happiness truly is will prevent us from investing a great deal of time and energy into pursuing something that isn't real. Happiness is a mental state, which means that it's something that takes time and practice to maintain. As a state, this also means that happiness, in and of itself, isn't a feeling. Rather, it consists of many positive feelings, such as joy, satisfaction, or contentment.

When psychologists use the term subjective well-being, they are referring to true or long-lasting happiness. This state arises when one feels an overall sense of contentment about one's life; it doesn't appear and disappear within a matter of moments. According to psychologists, subjective well-being has two core components: emotional balance and life satisfaction. Everyone experiences positive and negative emotions on a daily basis. Subjective well-being can be described as generally feeling more positive emotions than negative ones. Life satisfaction means feeling generalized contentment with *all* areas of your life, including relationships, work, and achievements.

Subjective well-being is treated by happiness researchers like any other psychological "diagnosis." It comes with a list of "symptoms" to give psychologists a clear and common understanding of what researchers mean when they use the word "happiness." These "symptoms," however, are mostly a list of perceptions. Believing that you have accomplished what you wanted in life is one. Feelings of satisfaction with your life is another. In simple terms, the "signs and symptoms" of happiness are all related to one thing—believing that your life is good (Nelson-Coffey, 2020).

Scientists agree that about 40% of a person's overall happiness comes from their actions and thoughts, 50% is genetically determined, and just 10% is determined by the circumstances of your life. Since there's not much that can be done about genetics, the road to true happiness, then, is not good fortune or big accomplishments but through our habits and perceptions. True happiness is dependent on two factors: how you feel about your life overall and how you feel on a daily basis. Both of these things are largely dependent on both the patterns of our lives and the meaning that we assign to those patterns. Habits are the small, daily actions or thoughts that we have that make up the greater pattern of our lives. Positive habits will result in positive life patterns, ones that contribute to our overall happiness. Toxic or destructive habits, on the other hand, will inevitably result in destructive life patterns that eat away at our happiness, no matter what heights of success or good fortune we may reach (Bradberry, 2016).

Understanding this tells us that there are specific actions we can take to cultivate lasting happiness within our lives, including (Cherry, 2020):

Pursue Intrinsic Goals

Rather than the pursuit of extrinsic (or external) goals like wealth and status, research suggests that the pursuit of intrinsic goals is much more fulfilling. Achieving goals that you are internally and naturally motivated to pursue will leave you with a sense of pride and satisfaction that is a bit deeper and, therefore, more lasting.

Enjoy the Moment

Happiness researchers have also found that most people tend to over-earn. We become so focused on accumulating more material wealth that we forget to enjoy or appreciate the earnings we have.

Reframe Negative Thoughts

Happy people experience negative thoughts and feelings just as often as everyone else. The difference is that happy people don't get stuck in them, and these thoughts and feelings tend not to last as long. More depressive people, on the other hand, have what psychologists call a "negativity bias," or a tendency to experience the world from a negative viewpoint. Discounting the positive can have a real and lasting impact on the way we live our lives, influencing everything from how we make decisions to the way we view other people. If you're a naturally pessimistic person, then reframing your negative thoughts and feelings isn't an exercise in ignoring the bad parts of life. Rather, it's a way for you to overcome your negativity bias and achieve a more balanced view of the world.

The field of philosophy also has its own definition of happiness. The ancient Greek thinker Aristotle divided happiness into two distinct categories: hedonic and eudaimonic. Hedonic happiness is happiness that comes from pleasure. This kind of happiness comes from doing things that feel good, like self-care or fulfilling one's desires. This happiness is more fleeting or momentary.

Eudaimonic happiness, on the other hand, is a bit more long-lasting. This is the kind of happiness that comes from the pursuit of virtue or purpose. Eudaimonic happiness is characterized by the belief that your life has meaning and value. It's the kind of happiness that comes from doing things like fulfilling responsibilities or investing in long-term goals.

Studies have found that happy people tend to score extremely high when it comes to eudaimonic life satisfaction and higher than average when it comes to hedonic life satisfaction. This tells us that true happiness involves a little bit of both. Furthermore, each individual's understanding of which activities are hedonic and which are eudaimonic may be a little different. For example, most people might say that volunteering for a cause they are passionate about is more eudaimonic than hedonic. But if your volunteer work involves eating homemade cookies or cuddling with cute animals, then it might bring you a little bit of both (Cherry, 2020).

The presence of happiness in our lives doesn't just make us feel good. Psychologists have linked it with some real, measurable benefits in our lives (*Everything You Need to Know About Happiness in One Infographic*, n.d.):

- Happy people tend to be more successful across multiple areas of life, including marriage, friendship, and even income level.
- Happy people get sick less often, and when they do fall ill, they tend to experience fewer symptoms.
- Happy people tend to have more and better friends.
- Happy people donate more to charity (which, in turn, brings them even more happiness).
- Happy people are more helpful in both personal and professional situations.
- Happy people find it easier to overcome negative experiences like pain, sadness, or grief.
- Happy people tend to have a positive influence on others, bringing happiness into the lives of the people around them.
- Happy people tend to have deeper and more meaningful conversations.
- Happy people smile more, which has been linked with positive health benefits.
- Happy people both exercise more often and tend to have better diets.
- Happy people are more likely to feel content with what they have.
- Happy people tend to be healthier in the moment and tend to stay healthy longer in their lives.

- Believe it or not, happy people have also been found to live longer.
- And, of course, happy people tend to have better overall mental health.

But the most important takeaway from all this research is this: You CAN change your happiness. It's not a fixed state. It's not something that you're born with. It's not a personality trait or an inheritance. It's something that anyone can achieve and maintain on their own regardless of the circumstances of their lives.

I don't need scientific studies to show me how true this is. I experienced it myself. For years, I was trapped in some pretty bad life circumstances. I had a terrible marriage and a terrible job with a demanding and exhausting schedule. But at long last, I managed to free myself from both of these circumstances by traveling all the way across the country to start a new life on the West Coast.

If happiness was entirely dependent on external circumstances, this would be the end of my story. And it's true, my situation in California was much better than the one I had left behind. I had the chance to completely start over, to be anyone I wanted to be. I made new friends. I found a good job with reasonable hours. And yet, after about a year, I found myself feeling just as miserable as I had been before I moved.

When I realized this, I discovered something incredibly important. By "starting my life over," all I had managed to do was change the *external* circumstances of my life. But I had done nothing to change who I was on the inside. I realized that I still had many negative patterns of thoughts and behavior that were damaging my mental health and that had damaged my mental health even when my life circumstances were bad. Getting away from my abusive partner and terrible job was only the first step. It had given me the opportunity to see what the *real* problems were.

For the rest of this book, I will walk you through the negative thoughts and habits that I discovered were destroying my happiness and provide you with practical solutions for changing them so that you, too, can discover that simple truth I learned so many years ago. Happiness, as it turns out, doesn't come from outside us; it comes from *within*.

Chapter 3:

Happiness Starts From Within

Very little is needed to make a happy life; it is all within yourself, in your way of thinking.

- Marcus Aurelius Antoninus

To find internal happiness, we have to take a moment to consider where true happiness comes from. Does it come from being loved, eating good food, or having a great body? The answer, unfortunately, is no. Even things like being loved by another aren't sources of long-lasting happiness. These things can cause brief moments of hedonic happiness. But true happiness, ultimately, isn't about momentary, hedonic experiences. It's about allowing these brief, pleasurable moments to lead us toward happiness and appreciation for life itself. And the real secret to true happiness is learning how to have little moments of pleasure even when there are no pleasurable stimuli around you.

There are plenty of things going on inside of us that can bring happiness. Your own generosity or love is just as beautiful and wonderful as a good cup of coffee or a gorgeous sunset. If we learn to notice and appreciate the beauty within ourselves, then we can find happiness no matter what is happening around us. This doesn't mean that we stop appreciating the good things happening in our lives, but it does mean that we stop being dependent on those things for our happiness.

So, as you continue to experience the world beyond this book, pay attention to what's around you. Notice the food you eat, the coffee or water that you drink in the morning. Is there anything good about them? Anything that can be appreciated? What about in the room around you? Or in the book you're reading?

Once you start paying attention, it will be hard to stop. You'll quickly learn that you are surrounded by beauty, creativity, and inspiration, often in places that you never thought to look for these things before. Awareness and mindfulness exercises are designed to help us pay closer attention to the world around us and, therefore, make it easier for us to think in happier and more optimistic ways. Although it can sometimes seem otherwise, the human brain is wired for happiness. And regardless of genetics, it is possible to overcome a biological predisposition for depression with experience and practice. The ability for the brain to change the way that it's naturally wired is called *neuroplasticity,* and it's what makes it possible for those who are vulnerable to depression to achieve lasting happiness (Baubata, 2019).

Self-Acceptance

Happiness and self-acceptance go hand-in-hand. In fact, your level of self-acceptance determines your level of happiness. The more self-acceptance you have, the more happiness you'll allow yourself to accept, receive, and enjoy. In other words, you enjoy as much happiness as you believe you're worthy of.

- Robert Holden

Happiness, ultimately, cannot be dependent on external validation. So the first step in setting yourself up for happiness is learning how to accept yourself for who you are, warts and all. This positive cognitive habit is arguably the most powerful when it comes to cultivating inner happiness and is also probably the one that contemporary humans practice the least. So if this sounds like something that you need to work on, then you are far from alone.

True self-acceptance is unconditional. It's about being aware of your own strengths and weaknesses, without judging or denying parts of yourself. Self-acceptance is related to self-esteem, but the two are slightly different concepts. Self-esteem is essentially how valuable you believe yourself to be. Self-acceptance, on the other hand, is about completely accepting yourself as you are, not as you should or could be. When we practice self-acceptance, we embrace all sides of ourselves. We learn to admit and accept not just the things that are good but also the things about ourselves that we think are bad, ugly, or shameful. True self-acceptance ultimately teaches us to love all parts of ourselves, even our flaws.

But how does self-acceptance influence our happiness? According to some, self-acceptance and happiness are two words for the same thing. It's difficult to be unhappy if you accept and love yourself. The trick, however, is learning to love *all* of yourself. It's easy to love yourself when life is going well or when you accomplish one of your goals. But self-acceptance is about learning to love yourself no matter what. It's much harder to love or forgive yourself after you fail or make a mistake. But if you can learn unconditional self-acceptance, then you will learn to embrace unconditional happiness. If you love and accept yourself fully, then your happiness will no longer be dependent on or even affected by whether or not the people around you like you. Your joy will be based on who you are, not on what you do.

But how do we find self-acceptance? Self-acceptance is not a feeling or even a mental state; it's a skill. And like any skill, it takes time and practice before you get really good at it. Some people are taught self-acceptance at a young age, and so, like children who take music lessons or play sports from a young age, it's much easier for them to accept themselves as adults. Others will encounter self-acceptance for the first time as adults, and so, like someone who is learning a foreign language for the first time, it's going to be slow and strange and frustrating at first. That's okay!

One incredibly useful tool for finding self-acceptance is meditation. There are hundreds of guided meditations available on the internet that focus specifically on self-acceptance. *Calm* and other meditation apps can help you to easily make meditation a part of your daily routine and help you to pick specific meditations based on whatever mental skill you are currently working on.

Many people who struggle with self-acceptance are also burdened by negative thoughts. Psychologists often refer to our negative thought voice as our *inner critic*. This is that little voice inside your head that's constantly telling you that you aren't good enough. It's the voice that tells you you're not attractive enough, adequate enough, or smart enough (Farewell, 2016).

It may seem like the right thing to do is to simply ignore this voice. But the best way to challenge your inner critic is to engage it in conversation. For example, imagine that you just submitted a project proposal to your boss, and she rejected it. Your inner critic will probably tell you that your boss was right to reject it. It will start to criticize, judge, or blame you. Do any of these thoughts sound familiar?

- *Wow, you really screwed that one up.*
- *You knew she'd reject it. I don't know why you even submitted it in the first place.*
- *You're so bad at this job! You're lucky she didn't fire you!*

When these thoughts start to arise, speak to your inner critic as if it were another person. Say something like,

"Actually, I think this was a really interesting proposal." If you have a strong inner critic, this probably won't be enough. It may come back with something like, "Interesting? It wasn't what she was looking for at all! You'd better start cleaning out your locker now while you still have time."

But when these thoughts arise, challenge them again. If your inner critic starts inventing terrible future situations or consequences for very small or normal mistakes, challenge it. Say something like, "You're making a lot of assumptions." Or even better, "Why are you so angry about this?"

Conversations like this with yourself might make you feel a bit crazy at first, but you'll probably find them to be extremely therapeutic. Learning to challenge your negative thoughts the moment they arise will help you to see that your inner critic's voice is not the voice of reason or reality. To take this one step further, you can write out your responses to your inner critic in your journal or record the entire conversation on paper. To slowly start to replace the voice of your inner critic, practice using self-talk that is kind and compassionate.

Meditation and working with your inner critic, however, are just two things you can try for cultivating self-acceptance. Here are a few more simple thought exercises you can work into your daily routine to start learning to love and accept yourself as you are.

Cultivate Self-Compassion

Refrain, as much as you can, from judging yourself or identifying with negative self-beliefs.

Celebrate Your Strengths and Accept Your Weaknesses

Make a list of your strengths if you have trouble noticing them.

Surround Yourself With People Who Accept You

People who cause you to doubt or feel bad about yourself are not people who are going to bring you happiness.

Cultivating Happy Habits

Self-acceptance is just one of many mental skills you can develop that positive psychologists call "happy habits." These run in opposition to the toxic mental habits that we discussed in chapter 1. For example, practicing self-acceptance makes you less likely to compare yourself to others. When viewed from this angle, we can think of happiness not as a mental state but as a lifestyle. It's the inevitable result of a combination of beneficial habits that all work together to create the overall life-state we call "happiness." If we work to introduce happy habits into our lives, then we have no room for toxic habits and, therefore, become less vulnerable to negative moods like depression or anxiety.

To determine which happy habits are most common in our society, a charity organization called Action for Happiness conducted a survey of 5,000 people, asking them to rate how often they practiced different habits on a scale of 1 to 10. Participants rated 10 happy habits in total. The 10 habits used in the survey came from the Ten Keys to Happier Living Framework developed by Action for Happiness. These habits are (University of Hertfordshire, 2014):

- Giving or doing things for others
- Relating or connecting with other people
- Exercising and/or generally taking care of the body
- Appreciating or noticing the world around you
- Trying out or learning new things
- Direction or setting goals for yourself
- Resilience or finding ways to bounce back from negative situations
- Emotion or taking a positive approach to life
- Acceptance or being comfortable with who you are
- Meaning or becoming part of something bigger than yourself

According to this survey, *giving* was the habit that participants practiced the most. This habit got an average score of 7.41 out of 10. About 36% of respondents, however, gave this habit a score of 8 or 9. Number two was *relating*. This habit got an average score of 7.36.

When asked how often they performed *acceptance* in their daily lives, respondents gave this habit an average performance score of just 5.56 out of 10. Just 5% of respondents gave *acceptance* a perfect 10, meaning that just 5% of respondents practiced self-acceptance on a daily basis.

The total results of the survey were (University of Hertfordshire, 2014):

- Giving - 7.41
- Relating - 7.36
- Exercising - 5.88
- Appreciating - 6.57
- Trying out - 6.26
- Direction - 6.08
- Resilience - 6.33
- Emotion - 6.74
- Acceptance - 5.56
- Meaning - 6.38

This study reveals some interesting things about our socio-cultural understanding of what happiness is and how to achieve it. According to this study, the happy habit people are most likely to engage in is giving to others. And while there's certainly nothing wrong with this, it seems that self-acceptance is something most of us struggle with. When we look at what's going on in our society to create this poverty of self-acceptance, it makes sense.

Our world puts a great deal of pressure on us to be successful, which inevitably leads to the toxic habit of comparing ourselves with others. But, as this and other research suggests, if we can learn to be more accepting of ourselves, we may find that our levels of unhappiness and anxiety greatly decrease. The way that we view ourselves has a huge impact on how happy and satisfied we are with our lives. And while most of us are pretty good at doing simple actions (like giving) that bring us happiness, we're unskilled at building habits that bring more long-lasting satisfaction (acceptance).

So how do we build a daily practice of self-acceptance? Researchers at Action for Happiness recommended three simple exercises (University of Hertfordshire, 2014).

Be as Kind to Yourself as You Are to Others

If you make a mistake, try to see it as an opportunity to learn and grow. If you do something well, no matter how small, notice it and appreciate yourself for it.

Ask a Close Friend to Tell You What They Think Your Strengths Are

You may be surprised by what they say. Knowing your strengths will make it much easier for you to accept your flaws.

Get Enough Alone Time

Spending time alone gives you a moment to tune in to yourself and make peace with your feelings.

Self-acceptance is the first, and arguably the most important, of the happy habits. It's about becoming aware of your strengths and weaknesses and, therefore, cultivating a more realistic understanding of your talents and capabilities. But the part of self-acceptance that leads to happiness is developing a feeling of satisfaction with yourself as you are regardless of your flaws or mistakes (Seltzer, 2008).

Gratitude

Another important happy habit is **gratitude.** Gratitude is strongly associated with happiness in positive psychology research, and there are a number of studies that prove the connection. For example, a 2002 study found that people who are faced with adversity or even trauma are significantly more resilient if they practice gratitude than people who don't. Another 2010 study found that victims of interpersonal offenses had increased cardiovascular strength immediately after the incident if they were able to practice gratitude for the lessons learned or how they survived the incident (Stoerkel, 2020).

Practicing gratitude involves much more than just saying thank you. It's about showing an appreciation for life itself and, therefore, not taking anything for granted. People who focus on what they are grateful for have been found to have much lower rates of depression, are more adaptive, and even have stronger social relationships.

Another recent study asked participants to journal for 10 to 20 minutes before bed every night. Participants were divided into three groups. One group was asked to write about the hassles and struggles they experienced during the day, one was asked to write about neutral or routine events, and one was asked to write about the things they were grateful for. The study found that the gratitude group reported significantly higher levels of positive emotions, subjective happiness, and overall life satisfaction than the other groups (Cherry, 2020).

And it's not just science that recognizes the power of gratitude. According to the Dalai Lama, gratitude is a core tenet of Tibetan Buddhism. The key to contentment, he teaches, is to feel grateful for the things that you already have (Robinson, 2019).

Some practical exercises you can try to cultivate a daily gratitude habit are (*Gratitude and Happiness,* 2020):

A Daily Gratitude Journal

Every day, make a list of four or five things that you are grateful for. The more comfortable you get with this exercise, the more you'll start to find that five feels like a very small number.

Gratitude Game

In this game, everyone sits in a circle, with one person designated the leader. The leader begins with the sentence "I am grateful for…" and chooses something that begins with the letter A. The next person completes the sentence with something that begins with the letter B. Continue to move around the circle, with each person naming something they are grateful for until you have gone through the entire alphabet.

Write a Thank-You Note

Psychologists at the University of Pennsylvania recently conducted a study on 411 people. The goal was to compare the impact of different psychological interventions on the participants' happiness. The study found that when participants were asked to write a thank-you note and deliver it to someone, their happiness scores increased significantly. This, in fact, was the most successful intervention in the entire study, with results lasting up to a month after the exercise had been completed (Harvard Health Publishing, 2011).

Thank Someone Mentally

This can be anyone—a teacher, friend, or parent. Spend a few minutes reflecting on the ways that they have helped you or made your life better. Then, have an imaginary conversation with this person. Tell them how you feel, and thank them mentally for improving your life in the ways that they have. If you're still in contact with this person, you can choose to take your mental exercise into real life if you wish (Greenberg, 2015).

Count Your Blessings

Similar to keeping a gratitude journal, make a list at the end of each day of all the blessings you received that day. Your list can be as short as one or as long as 100.

Pray

For those who are religious, it's probably true that you find yourself praying most when bad things happen. But praying when *good* things are happening can be an incredibly powerful spiritual practice.

Meditation

Meditation doesn't just help with self-acceptance. There are hundreds of guided meditations out there on the internet that focus on the practice of gratitude as well.

Think of (and Thank) a Person Who Has Helped You

Once you've chosen your person, spend a week simply noticing how they make your life better. At the end of the week, make a plan to do something special for them to demonstrate just how much you appreciate them.

Optimism

Our next happy habit is **optimism.** Optimism is the mental skill of responding to problems with confidence and belief in oneself. Optimistic people believe that negative events are both temporary and limited in their scope (Martin, 2019).

Becoming more optimistic will increase your ability to handle stressful situations, which has the added benefit of reducing the harmful effects of stress on your body. When we think optimistically about the future, it allows us to feel excited about the things that are coming our way. Excitement allows us to enjoy positive events before they've even happened, doubling our happiness and increasing the joy of our experience. Our happiness lasts much longer if we are happy before, during, and after the experience of good times (Singh, 2019).

Optimism has also been found to increase motivation, which, in turn, increases productivity. Optimism gives you the bravery you need to go out and try for the things that you really want out of life. The ability to imagine yourself getting what you want is the first step in achieving it (*Positive thinking: Optimism, gratitude, and happiness,* 2017).

Optimism even has benefits for your physical health. Studies have shown that optimistic people tend to have better cardiovascular and immune function. In fact, optimism is one of the strongest predictors of cardiovascular disease. Optimistic people tend to have much better cholesterol levels and generally live longer than people who identify as cynical (Scott, 2020).

Some practical exercises you can try to cultivate a daily habit of optimism are:

Try on a Positive Lens

Don't wait passively for good thoughts to come. Make an active effort to shift your perspective by thinking good thoughts.

Connect With People Who Make You Smile

Research shows that we are happiest when we are around other happy people. Make an effort to spend time with more people who are optimistic, and their positivity will eventually rub off on you (Goldsmith, 2020).

Acknowledge What You Can (and Cannot) Control

Optimistic people are not only able to adapt; they also thrive in the face of uncertainty. This is because optimism gives us a more realistic understanding of what we can and cannot control in any given situation. If you lose your job, for example, you cannot control that you were let go. What you can control is whether or not you start looking for a new job. Optimism prevents us from ruminating or obsessing over daily stressors that are out of our control. When we ruminate, we are focused on what could have or should have been, not on what is. Optimism helps us to remain focused on the present and, therefore, empowers us to seize opportunities and make positive changes in our lives (Steinhilber, 2017).

Acknowledge the Negative

This may sound like a strange way to cultivate optimism, but optimism isn't about ignoring or denying the negative. In fact, refusing to acknowledge the negative aspects of life can be just as dangerous as refusing to acknowledge the positive. You may be focused on getting a better job or finding a romantic partner, but if you don't acknowledge the very real obstacles in your path, then you won't have the skills you need to confront them. Optimism is really the art of balanced thinking, a way for us to see both the positive and the negative in the world around us. This is what makes optimism more realistic than pessimism, which refuses to acknowledge the good things in life. Optimism allows us to accept everything for what it is and take the right steps to make positive change.

Visualize Your Best Possible Self

Imagine a future world in which everything happens exactly the way you want it to. This can be short term (imagine that your project is successful or that everyone likes it) or long term (imagine yourself achieving your dreams or your major life goals).

Smash Your Pessimistic Thoughts

Keep a small rock or crystal in your pocket or purse. Whenever you find yourself thinking negative thoughts, touch the rock and imagine yourself physically smashing the negative thoughts with it (White & White, 2014).

Give Positive Feedback

Believe it or not, giving compliments is an excellent way to practice optimism. Acknowledging the good in another person not only trains you to look for good things in the people around you, but it also improves the quality of your relationships with others.

Practice Gratitude

It's difficult to be optimistic without feeling some kind of appreciation for the people who have helped you along the way. When you're optimistic, you tend to notice all of the wonderful things the people around you do to make your life a little better (Morin, 2020). On the flip side, if you're struggling to think positively, one easy way to give yourself a boost is to take a look at your life. What are you grateful for? Who are you grateful for?

Resilience

Resilience is a happy habit that is sometimes called "mental toughness." This is the art of being happy when you're faced with a difficult or negative situation.

Believe it or not, research shows us that people who have experienced some adversity in their lives are generally happier than people who have never experienced adversity. Though no one wants bad things to happen, overcoming challenges is what shapes our identities and gives us the skills we need to cope with stressors. Without these skills, even the smallest bumps in the road can destroy our emotional well-being (*Everything you need to know about happiness in one infographic,* n.d.).

Some exercises you can try to build emotional resilience are:

Accept What You Can and Can't Control

As with optimism, the first step in cultivating resilience is getting a realistic view of what you can and can't control about your situation. Research tells us that people who focus on what they can change are better able to navigate difficult situations than people who focus on the things that put them in the bad situation to begin with. If you focus on actions you can take to get yourself out of a bad place, then you'll be more likely to mitigate the negative effects when bad things happen. Furthermore, engaging in actions for positive change makes you feel better and can even increase your productivity (Markman, 2018).

Reach Out to Other People

The last thing we want to do when disaster strikes is be social. But reaching out to others is one of the best things you can do when you're feeling sad or stressed. Social engagement is a critical component of building resilience. If you talk about what's making you feel sad or anxious, you'll probably find that the people around you have had similar experiences. Sadness has a way of making you feel isolated and alone. Reaching out to others is a way to confirm that your situation is not unique and that you have a support system ready to help you when things get tough.

Get the Easy Win

When you experience a loss in one area of life, you're likely to start looking for flaws and negatives in other parts of your life. So if you've just experienced a setback, try not to start a long-term project or take on a responsibility that's difficult or stressful. Instead, find something that you can complete with ease. Achieving a little victory will remind you that one big setback doesn't have to impact the rest of your life.

Think Well of Others

Actively try to find a good reason behind other people's actions, even when those actions are annoying or hurtful. If you're feeling angry or frustrated, you tend to assume that the people around you are behaving in an aggressive or oppressive way. These feelings can be particularly potent when you are passed over for a big opportunity. Remind yourself that most of the people around you are not out to get you. Just because someone did something that held you back doesn't mean that they want you to fail or that they did it on purpose.

Allow Yourself to Feel Unpleasant Emotions

To find true resilience, you have to get comfortable feeling all of your feelings, including the ones that are unpleasant. Suppressing your painful feelings will ultimately cause you to stifle your positive ones as well. Your brain doesn't distinguish between positive and negative, good or bad. All of our emotions come from the same source. If you give yourself permission to feel your negative emotions, you'll find that you have much easier access to the positive ones as well. Furthermore, once you become aware of your feelings, you can take action to respond to them in an appropriate way (Cabelly, 2016).

Choose How You Respond

No matter how powerless we may feel, we always have a choice. Every action that we take is a choice that we make in the moment. We can choose to take life for granted or to practice gratitude every day. We can choose to look at our failures as catastrophes, or we can choose to see adversity as an opportunity for learning and growth.

Change Your Story

A core facet of resilience is learning how to change your story. What do you tell others about your life? Do you present yourself to others or yourself as a failure? A success? Constantly telling stories about how you are struggling or about your past failures creates the danger of developing a victim mentality. Don't be the victim; be the underdog. Stop reliving your awkward and embarrassing moments. Choose to rewrite those moments as stories of your triumph, your bravery, and your ability to change and learn from difficult situations (Nyx, 2020).

Knowing Your Values

Last but certainly not least is the happy habit of **knowing your values.** Values are the things that you believe to be true and fair about the world. The more your actions honor your values, the happier you will become. When we move through life without honoring or even knowing our values, we start to lose our sense of self. By identifying or reaffirming your values, you can take real steps to bring your life more closely in alignment with the things you believe are most important (Goldsmith, 2012).

If you're not sure what your values are, start with this list (Davis, 2018):

- Authenticity
- Adventure
- Balance
- Bravery
- Compassion
- Challenge
- Citizenship
- Community
- Creativity
- Curiosity
- Determination
- Fairness
- Freedom
- Friendships
- Fun
- Generosity
- Growth
- Honesty
- Integrity
- Justice
- Kindness
- Knowledge
- Leadership
- Learning
- Love
- Loyalty

- Openness
- Optimism
- Recognition
- Respect
- Responsibility
- Security
- Self-respect
- Social connection
- Spirituality
- Stability
- Status
- Wisdom

Take a moment to circle the three values that are most important to you. Now take a look at your life. What do you do on a daily basis that brings you into alignment with these values? What do you do that is at odds with these values? How can you change the actions that violate your values?

Chapter 4:

Indulging Your Passions and Interests

There's no doubt that introducing happy habits into your life will greatly improve your well-being. But habits are just one element of true happiness. Habits are the ways that we grow and maintain our happiness, but passions and interests are the things that make us feel most alive. Indulging in your passions is a huge happiness booster as it can help you feel more engaged with yourself and the world around you. Passions give you a reason to keep learning and something to work toward. They give you something in common with other people and can make it easier to form lasting social connections. Passions like rock climbing, fly fishing, or even knitting often have beneficial physical components that enrich our bodies as well as our minds. Passion also gives meaningful structure to the way you spend your time. Living life according to your passions makes the world seem like a richer and much more interesting place (Rubin, 2017).

When you're in pain, your passions can become a place of refuge, a place you can retreat to for distraction or solace. As such, the pursuit of your passion greatly reduces stress levels and dramatically increases your overall happiness. One recent study found that participants who engaged in hobbies had 34% lower stress levels and 14% lower sadness levels than people who didn't.

Finding and indulging in a passion can transform your life. Passions reveal hidden truths about who we truly are and provide us with a sense of purpose. Best of all, passions are things that we engage in purely for ourselves or for others and not for the expectation of some kind of payoff.

A passion doesn't have to be something you are certified in or even very good at. The happiness that we derive from passions comes from the simple joy of engaging in the activity itself. Passions can also change over time. Certain circumstances, maturity, and life situations can introduce us to new passions or cause old passions to fade. That's okay! Following your passions means doing what's right for you at the time and nothing more or less.

But what if you aren't sure what your passions are? Too often, people struggle to find their passions because they get stuck pursuing the passions that they think they should have rather than pursuing the things that genuinely bring them joy. Often, we are taught from a young age what our passions or interests "should" be, and it can sometimes be painful for us to admit that these are not the things that bring us true happiness.

Too many of us go through a significant portion of our lives assuming that something is our passion without bothering to look at it too closely. When we fail to achieve greatness, we start to blame ourselves.

You might just think that you're lazy or not as smart or talented as other people. And if you don't want to talk about or practice or engage in your passion all the time, you don't beat yourself up. If you'd rather watch the baseball game than practice for your upcoming recital, what's the problem, right? Aren't you allowed to take a break once in a while?

Passions are different from careers. Passions are things that we *love*, that we are so consumed by that they never feel like a chore or a bore. You don't have to make your passion your career to be happy. But it is important to be honest with yourself about what your true passions are so that you can make time for them. If your passion is learning new things, you can do that anytime and anywhere. If your passion is clothes, you don't have to become a fashion designer or critic. You can take pride and joy in developing your own personal and unique style, whether you're working a desk job or raising children or doing anything else during the day.

Think of how many artists have "day jobs." They are able to find happiness and meaning in their work because they choose jobs that fit into their passions rather than choosing passions that fit in with their jobs. Even the most boring desk job can be fulfilling if you know that you're there to facilitate your writing or painting career.

Whether you transform your hobby into a career or simply turn to it as a way to relieve stress, indulging in your passions is a necessary and beneficial form of self-care. For another example of how important finding and honoring our passions can be, take a look at the story of Andrew Rea. Today, he has an extremely popular YouTube channel called *Binging with Babish*. But just six months before he started this channel, he was crippled by depression. He knew his true passions were food and filmmaking, but his day job as a visual effects supervisor only seemed to nurture one. Rea began filming his cooking videos at night after work as a way to blow off steam and have some fun. Getting himself cooking again brought joy back into his life and gave him something to look forward to at night when he got off work (Schumer, 2018).

Rea's videos weren't created to transform his career; they were created to transform his life on a very small, daily basis. This is the power of honoring your passions; they bring a spark to your life that enables you to do great things and to combat the inevitable depression that comes when we fail to engage with the things we love the most.

Finding Your Passion

So what exactly is passion? *Merriam-Webster* defines "passion" as "a strong feeling of enthusiasm or excitement for something, or about doing something."

Passion can be a good feeling, but we can hate with passion just as easily as we can love (*Finding your passion is one major key in happiness*, 2021).

While passions often consume us, they can become dangerous if they become obsessive. Obsession happens when we think or engage with one thing and one thing only to the exclusion of all else. This kind of behavior is illogical and destructive. Rather than indulging in joy-giving passions, we are allowing our emotions to control and override our logical thinking. When a passion becomes an obsession, it stops bringing us joy and starts bringing us pain and turmoil.

It's also important to remember that passions and careers are not the same thing. But with the prevalence of social and internet media, it's too easy to look at movie stars, travel bloggers, and other glamorous people as examples of what "passion" really looks like. But just because someone is more visible doesn't mean they have more passion. And just because someone plays music for a living doesn't necessarily mean that music is their passion or that the way they've chosen to pursue that passion is the only legitimate path.

Though passion is quite a dramatic word, the feeling that we get when we indulge in our passions is quite tranquil. Inner happiness is subtle. If your passion is your home environment, you don't have to engage in large-scale home improvements. Small changes in decoration, layout, or even the simple maintenance of a snug and cozy home can fill you with joy just as surely as a big, impressive project.

Throughout our lives, it's possible for passions to change completely, especially when we reach a certain stage or achieve a certain goal. Imagine that your passion was baseball, but then you decide to study business and leave baseball behind. The choice to major in business came from a shift in interests. Perhaps you won a major championship in high school or college, and now you're ready to move on to bigger and better things. Deciding to leave something that consumed your life before is hardly a betrayal of self. Instead, it's a conscious choice to discover something new about yourself.

So knowing all this, how in the world does one discover and honor their passion? How can you indulge in your passions without going overboard? How can you make time for your passions without dropping your daily responsibilities?

To get you started thinking about your passions, try making a vision board. This is a simple activity you can try to get yourself thinking about your life in a new way.

Creating a Vision Board

One exercise you can do to help reconnect you with your passions is creating a vision board. This technique is sometimes called a "dream" or "motivation" board as well. Your vision board can be physical or digital, whichever is more convenient for you. It can be any size, from a huge poster board to a small piece of printer paper. There is no right or wrong way to create a vision board. The important thing to keep in mind is that it's something you're going to look at every day, something that will be designed to bring you inspiration for the things that you genuinely like (*Finding your passion is one major key in happiness*, 2021).

Start by taking a moment to think about the things that you like, the things that excite you the most. Do you love listening to music? Does the idea of having your own crafting room or studio space excite you? Is there a certain cause or political issue that you feel strongly about? Do you dream about travel? Have you been saving up for a classic or vintage car? Anything that fills you with positive emotions is appropriate for the vision board.

Whatever you choose, the images that you pin to the board should be ones that fill you with inspiration, that remind you of what your passions and goals are. You can use words or pictures or even make a digital board if that's easier for you. For example, if your passion is camping, you may want to fill your board with pictures of trees and forests. You could include photos of yourself camping in the past or a cartoon image of a tent. Anything that reminds you of the things that you love and the goals that you have is appropriate for the board.

Your vision board can be more than just a reminder of your passions. It can be a way for you to actively bring more of your passions into your life. Perhaps you haven't been camping as much because of a physical injury or because your current job doesn't give you enough vacation time. You could put pictures on the board that remind you of recovery or images that inspire you to go out and find a new job. Your passion is what fills you with joy at the thought of camping. And your images of recovery or job hunting are reminders of how doing those less pleasant things will ultimately lead to more time and energy for the things that you love most. And if you're not sure what your "passion" is, just focus on filling the vision board with things that you love, and see if you notice a pattern or theme emerge.

Let Your Passions Bring You Happiness

Don't overthink it. Instead, let happiness itself guide you toward your passions. If you suddenly find your spirits lifted and your energy level increasing, make a mental note. What were you doing that made you feel so happy and satisfied? Perhaps you never saw your volunteer work at the clinic or your part-time job at the local animal shelter as a passion. No matter what it is, you can always justify carving time out of your day for something that meets your needs and lifts your spirits (*Find a passion that makes you happy*, 2016).

Passions are what bring us lasting happiness, but ironically, we often feel discouraged or embarrassed about pursuing them. When it comes to pursuing things, on the other hand, we find ways to legitimize and justify our efforts. The same person that brags about saving for a new car or a down payment on a home may feel strangely shy about admitting that they spent the morning reading or playing the piano. Worse, our materialistic culture can often convince us that sacrificing the time we might spend practicing the piano to make more money to buy the house is what will bring us *real* happiness. But the exact opposite is true. Things bring us fleeting happiness. Sure, they make our lives easier, but they don't bring us deep and lasting joy.

Passions, on the other hand, can be built into the very fabric of our lives. Passions connect us with a sense of purpose. They make us feel more connected to ourselves and the world around us when they are done for the simple joy of it. So if you love playing the piano, don't stop playing just because you have no plans to become a concert pianist. Just give yourself 15 minutes in the evening to play and enjoy the deep, long-lasting boost in happiness and well-being that comes with such a practice (Neilson, 2018).

When looking for your passions, don't look at your certifications or even your talents. You may be naturally good with numbers or find it easy to put new things together, but that doesn't necessarily mean you have a passion for math or engineering. Passions are things that make you purely happy, plain and simple. There's no need to justify, modify, or commodify them if doing so will diminish the joy you get from them (*Adventskalender 2020/Rituals/Exclusieve kerstkalender*, 2020).

Positive psychologists have done a great deal of research on passions and hobbies, and the results of their research might surprise you (*Infographic: How our hobbies make us happier*, 2020).

Studies suggest that we get the most personal satisfaction from activities that we've chosen for ourselves rather than ones that have been assigned to us. One study found that the three basic elements needed for a hobby to be fully satisfying are:

1. Learning or developing a skill,
2. Spending time with others, and
3. Improving the lives of others.

On the other hand, people who filled their leisure time with escapist activities like shopping or drinking were found to be less fulfilled, less healthy, and more easily bored.

If you're like most Americans, then according to one study, you have an average of five hours and five minutes of leisure time every day (including the weekends). That's a lot of time! Devoting that time to your passions has been found to prevent depression and other mental health issues. And if you have some extra cash, another study found that spending money on experiences tended to make people happier in the long run than spending money on material objects (Life, 2018).

Hobbies

But not everything you do in your free time has to be related to your passion. Hobbies, whether we do them as relaxing activities or turn them into careers, have real, measurable benefits as well. Hobbies offer us an important break from other aspects of our life that may be stressful, such as work or raising children. This is why many people find themselves in search of new hobbies after they've transformed an old hobby into a career. Doing something professionally is often much more stressful than doing it for fun. The ideal hobbies are stimulating for both body and mind but not too stressful or demanding.

Hobbies also offer us new challenges and opportunities to learn things about ourselves. This, in turn, offers us opportunities to improve ourselves, increases our patience with ourselves and others, and makes us more mindful by keeping us fully engaged in the present moment. Hobbies can also be a vehicle through which we expand our social circle by giving us the opportunity to meet like-minded people and share our passions with others (Cudmore, 2019).

If you're searching for some ideas, here are a few different hobbies you can try as well as the benefits they've been found to incur (*Infographic: How our hobbies make us happier*, 2020):

Hobbies: Creative and Classic

One study found that **taking photos** might increase our enjoyment of our experiences. The study found that people who took photos were *more* engaged with their positive experiences than people who didn't.

Singing with others, such as in a choir or with a band, has been found to significantly increase rates of happiness. And whether it's your passion or not, singing has also been linked to improved immune system function.

Writing or journaling about positive experiences has been linked to all kinds of mental health benefits. But another study also found that those who wrote about negative experiences had increased resilience and were able to navigate negative life situations more easily.

A recent prison study found that **painting** and drawing every day helped inmates to feel they had more control over their lives and significantly increased their mood. While this was true for all genders, the study found that the mood boost connected with art was much higher in female participants than in men.

Reading literary fiction has been found to greatly increase our capacity for empathy. Unlike non-fiction, stories ask us to imagine and experience the inner lives of the characters, which is why they increase our ability to feel compassion for others (*Infographic: How our hobbies make us happier*, 2020).

Hobbies: Frivolous and Fun

Cooking is another hobby that's been extensively studied by happiness researchers. Many studies have demonstrated the positive mental health benefits of cooking and baking, in particular, which have been linked to a significant boost in confidence.

And if you want to just sit and do nothing for a bit, that's okay too. In fact, studies have found that **daydreaming** and engaging in unstructured free time boost creativity (*Infographic: How our hobbies make us happier*, 2020).

Hobbies: Challenging and Adventurous

Spending time outdoors every day has been linked to all kinds of positive benefits, including an improved ability to think clearly, higher creativity, more activity in the part of your brain that controls emotional stability, higher energy levels, and increased empathy for others. One study that compared **gardening** to reading in terms of stress reduction found that gardening came out on top (though reading was found to significantly reduce stress levels as well) (*Infographic: How our hobbies make us happier*, 2020).

Hobbies: Enriching and Inspiring

Yoga has also been connected to significant health benefits, including a significant boost in mood, improved brain function, and higher levels of overall happiness. **Tai chi**, a physical meditative practice with roots in China and Korea, has also been found to have many positive health benefits and is becoming more and more popular in Western nations. More and more studies in English are revealing that tai chi can significantly improve mental health and lower stress levels.

So no matter what your hobbies or passions are, there's a good chance that they don't just make you *feel* more alive; they may also be bringing very real benefits to your mind and body.

When you engage with your passions, you often enter a state of mind called the "flow" state. Sometimes this is referred to as being "in the zone." When you find yourself completely, enjoyably submerged in an activity, losing all sense of time, then you know you've found yourself a passion worth pursuing (*Everything you need to know about happiness in one infographic,* n.d.).

If you're still not sure what your passions are, here are a few more simple mind exercises you can try to bring more passion into your life.

Get to Know Yourself

Spend some time with yourself. Get to know what *your* values, beliefs, goals, dreams, joys, and fears are, not what you think they should be or what other people are telling you they are. When you're living a life that's true to who you are and what you want, you'll be able to feel it. Spending time with yourself will help you to discover the spark of passion. And when you do learn what your passions are, spending some time with yourself will help you to cultivate them without fear of judgment, at least in the beginning (Newsonen, 2014).

Understand What Your Passions Aren't

Whether you decide to try something new because it looks fun or because it'll be a career boost, trying new things is a good way to discover your passions. Opening yourself up to new experiences means stepping out of your comfort zone, which can be an extremely scary and difficult thing to do. But stepping out of your comfort zone will inevitably teach you a lot about yourself. Even if you don't find your passion, the things you learn about yourself (and sometimes, learning what you *don't* like) when you try new things will bring you ever closer to finding the things that you do love (Schumer, 2018).

Think Back to What You Enjoyed as a Child

While it's true that our passions can change with time, thinking back to what brought you joy as a child can sometimes give you clues as to what your passions might be as an adult. For example, perhaps you're no longer looking forward to hockey practice or robotics club as an adult. But think about *why* you enjoyed those activities so much. Try to find something as an adult that satisfies the same physical or social needs.

Keep Learning

Engaging in experiences that break you out of your comfort zone or teach you new skills will create opportunities for you to find new passions and learn new things along the way. One of the most effective ways to do this is to travel. Traveling to new places takes us out of our familiar world and puts us smack in the middle of an entirely new way of life. But if you don't have the money or vacation time to fly to a new country, just start with your own nation or even your own neighborhood. Walk down a street you've never been down, check out a museum or art gallery in the next town over, or try an international food you've never tried at a local restaurant (M, 2018).

Meet New and Exciting People

Often, we find new passions through other people. If the people around you aren't encouraging you to do things that you love, try finding another social group. It doesn't mean leaving your old friends behind. Just try signing up for a new club or inviting a coworker to lunch who you don't know very well. Maybe ask a friend to introduce you to one of their passions or invite you to a club that they regularly attend. You might not think that you'll enjoy knitting club or a poetry reading, but who better to introduce you than a friend you already know and trust?

Think About the Impact You Want to Have on the World

If you imagine yourself "changing the world," what's the first image that comes to mind? Is it planting a tree? Creating a great work of art? Saving lives as a surgeon or rescuing animals? Your idea of changing the world can give you insight as to what kind of impact you want to have on the world around you. The changes that you want to leave are related to your values, and your values can give you clues as to what kinds of activities will make you the happiest.

Use Your Skills in Different Ways

Perhaps you're a talented writer or you have a naturally green thumb. The obvious use of these skills would be to, well, write and garden, right? But try applying your skills in new or unexpected ways. If you're a writer, maybe try a new kind of writing, like legal or technical. Try writing erotica or start a blog. Applying your skills in new situations can help you to discover enjoyable and playful activities that may not have been available to you before you honed your skills.

Cultivate New Skills

Does your job offer professional development activities? Maybe there are free classes at the local library, or your friend just told you about the free app they've been using to learn Spanish. If something even remotely catches your interest, give it a try. Learning a new skill, especially one that you can apply to your career, can open up access to new activities, social opportunities, and even new people that you didn't have access to before. Spanish may not turn out to be your passion, but going to Spanish club after class may introduce you to a new group of friends, or Spanish cooking, or awaken you to Spanish dance, which may indeed turn out to be a passion of yours that you were just never exposed to before. And the worst case is that you learn a new skill that you can use to advance your career, which is hardly a bad thing!

When making time for your passions, look at your schedule in terms of weeks instead of days. Spend a week just tracking your life. See if there are any open spaces that you can conveniently fill with a passion or hobby. Once you've found your free hours, make a commitment to use that time for your passions. Making time for your passions might involve a small adjustment to your schedule, such as going to bed a little earlier so you can wake up before your children or partner. If you have children, see if you can adjust your schedule to get some time for yourself while they're at school or extracurricular activities (Schumer, 2018). No matter what, believe that indulging in your passions is an important and necessary part of your life.

However, enjoying your work doesn't necessarily mean getting paid for your passions. Getting paid to do something you love can change the way that you engage with it and sometimes create the need for new hobbies and passions (Iliff, 2015). Here are a few simple ways that you can inject more passion into your daily work and thereby bring some meaning and enjoyment to your workspace:

Engage Your Brain

More often than not, if you find yourself hating your job, it's because you're understimulated. One of the easiest and most effective ways you can find more joy in your work is to learn something new. Whether you sign up for a professional development course through your company or take a class on your own, make it your mission to learn a new skill that you can apply on the job. Not only will it make your work more enjoyable, but it will also probably improve your performance. As soon as you start learning something new, you'll probably find your job starts to become exciting again (Monster, n.d.).

Find Meaning

Think about the big picture around the work that you do individually. Studies have found that people are most productive at work when they feel that their actions are personally meaningful. What about your job appeals to your values? If you enjoy teaching or communicating, try to find ways to do more of those kinds of activities at work. If you value helping others, try to remind yourself of how your work contributes to a larger scheme. Think about why you took this job to begin with. Reminding yourself of your long-term goals can renew your sense of purpose during the day (Monster, n.d.).

Help Others

Feeling helpful and valued at work can significantly improve your experience. Being a mentor to someone younger or new to the company can rekindle your enthusiasm for your own job. See if your company has a mentoring program that you can sign up for. Volunteer to train new employees when they first arrive on the job.

Ask for More Responsibility

If you're feeling understimulated or undervalued, you may want to simply ask for more work. Is there a project that needs an extra hand? A department that's short-staffed? If you're tired of your job, asking for more work may be the last thing you feel like doing. But taking on new responsibilities can give you a new sense of purpose at work. Having and handling a new challenge may also change the way your supervisor or coworkers see you.

Re-Organize

Is your office or workspace neat and clean? Is your desk cluttered with knickknacks from vendors or stacks of old paperwork? And even if your physical space is neat and tidy, can you say the same for your computer? Getting rid of clutter has been proven to improve mental focus and productivity at work. But it's also been found to improve workplace happiness and satisfaction (Monster, n.d.).

Embrace Change

The average person changes careers multiple times before they retire. Even more people change companies within their chosen field or industry. Perhaps it's not the job that you hate but the company itself (Monster, n.d.).

Don't Be a Perfectionist

Perfectionism might appear to make you more productive, but it can seriously damage the quality of your work. Taking pride and giving your work your all is very different from obsessing over every detail. Rather than punishing or fearing mistakes, try learning from them. Allow yourself to take pleasure in your work, even if it's less than perfect (Belli, 2017).

Choose Your Coworkers Wisely

Perhaps it's not the job you hate but the people you work with. More importantly, maybe you love your coworkers, just not when they're at work. People who complain, are lazy, or are messy can start to drag you down with them. If at all possible, try to surround yourself with positive, passionate, and productive people while you're at work. Just as negative coworkers will start to tarnish your workday, positive coworkers will start to influence you with their good habits (Belli, 2017).

Chapter 5:

No Man Is an Island

While true happiness isn't dependent on other people, it's also true that sharing your happiness with others will only increase it. In fact, good social relationships are the number one predictor of happiness. In particular, the most important factor in living a happy life is having solid social support. These are the people you can lean on in times of trouble.

In some ways, the idea that positive social connections lead to happiness is common sense. Humans are social animals. To some degree, we require strong social connections to thrive. In fact, social connections are so important for our general wellness that some studies have suggested poor social interaction is a greater health risk than smoking (Kogan, 2013).

Happiness is a skill, one that becomes better with practice. But, like other skills, it's much easier and more pleasant to practice happiness with other people, especially those who are happy too. Sometimes, relationships can cause us trouble, drama, or pain, but overcoming social adversity increases our resilience and makes our relationships stronger. Good relationships certainly bring us more happiness than wealth, material things, or even successful careers because the people we are close to grow and change with us over time. Unlike money or physical objects, the people we are close to give back to us a portion of the love and care we invest in them. Often, they give us even more.

Studies have shown that people with strong social connections have much better physical and mental health than those who don't. They have lower rates of cardiovascular disease and better immune systems. And there are even studies to suggest that those with happy relationships tend to live longer than those who don't (DiGiulio, 2018).

Those who derive happiness from their relationships don't just keep that happiness contained within their social circle. Strong personal connections with coworkers make us more productive at work. Even one close relationship makes you more likely to help others and can be a predictor for volunteer work. On a similar note, people with strong social support are more likely to donate to charities than people who don't. Close social connections can even improve your brain function, making you a more creative problem-solver.

The urge to share positive experiences with others can also improve our overall happiness. Sharing positive moments with others increases our attention to the details of the moment. Wanting to share a happy moment with a loved one can also enhance our experience, prompting us to savor the moment ever more deeply. And the more deeply we savor positive experiences, the lower our levels of stress, guilt, and depression. Savoring positive experiences stimulates the part of the brain associated with happiness, and savoring those experiences with a loved one stimulates this part of the brain even more.

Happiness and positive social connections tend to feed off of one another. Happy people attract more good and positive people into their lives, which makes them even happier. Unhappy people, on the other hand, tend to find themselves struggling to maintain close friendships and, therefore, becoming more miserable.

Having a strong social network also increases your resilience in the face of adversity. Knowing that you aren't alone in your challenges often gives you the strength you need to face them. Overcoming adversity alone helps to shape our identities and strengthens us emotionally. But overcoming adversity with others often increases our ability to cope with future stressors. Overcoming challenges with others makes it easier for us to imagine a positive future, and it bonds us more closely with the people we care about (*Everything you need to know about happiness in one infographic,* 2020).

Studies have also shown that Americans who have strong religious or spiritual beliefs tend to be happier. However, upon closer examination, the *reason* that strong religious beliefs tend to make people happier is because of the strong social network that people get from their religion. Higher worship service attendance is directly correlated with stronger religious faith, and stronger religious faith has been found to be correlated with stronger feelings of compassion for others. The more compassionate we are, the more likely we are to offer emotional support to others. And the more emotional support we give to others, the happier we feel (Nelson-Coffey, 2020).

Religious or not, being connected to any kind of community helps to give us a sense of belonging, and this is crucial to developing feelings of happiness and overall well-being (Wingman Magazine, 2020). Local communities like neighborhood groups or community improvement projects are beneficial because they bring people together from many different backgrounds and give them the opportunity to bond through a shared experience or activity. Local communities also provide us with a much-needed support system that prevents us from feeling isolated or cutoff from the people around us (*Local Community*, 2020).

Spending quality time with loved ones is a direct path to happiness. One study found that people who spend six to seven hours a day with friends and family are 12 times more likely to report feeling happy as opposed to feeling stressed. And a study of people who work full-time found that participants experienced the most happiness on days when they spent eight to nine hours with family and friends.

Simply spending five minutes a day doing something nice for a loved one was found to have an instant and lasting positive effect on one's happiness. Thanking someone for something nice that they did for you has also been found to create a deep and lasting happiness boost. Studies have also shown that meaningful conversations with loved ones make us happier overall. Often, our happiest memories are ones that involve other people rather than things we experienced alone. One study even found that taking 30 seconds a day to help someone in need resulted in a happiness boost that lasted the rest of the day. This and other studies point to the fact that activities with a prosocial focus, such as helping others in need, have a significant impact on our happiness levels. Therefore, being of service, volunteering, or simply offering to help someone out won't just make you feel good; they're actively good for you too (Baltazzi, 2019).

If you are struggling to find ways to connect with others, here are a few simple ideas you can try (Santi, n.d.):

Give Your Time

The gift of time is often more valuable and more appreciated than the gift of money. You don't have to devote your entire life to a cause; even just a few hours a day or a few days a year can be enough to make a big difference in someone else's life as well as your own.

Give to Organizations

More specifically, give to organizations whose aims and results are both clear and transparent so that you can be sure that your money is truly going to a good cause.

Find Ways to Devote Your Interests and Skills

There's no reason that giving or serving others should have to feel like a sacrifice. Find ways to help others that are in alignment with your own interests, skills, and needs.

Be Proactive

Being cajoled or manipulated into giving doesn't make us feel good; in fact, it's quite the opposite. Giving to others to avoid humiliation or out of a sense of obligation is not only unhealthy, but it can also indicate problems with our relationships or even our self-esteem. Worse, feeling coerced into giving time, money, or energy that you don't have can trigger feelings of guilt and resentment. Instead, say no to things that aren't good or convenient for you, and actively look for ways to help others that feel more genuine.

Happiness Is Love

Relationships are connected to all of our strongest emotions. When they are positive and healthy, we feel much more happiness and contentment throughout our lives. But when they are toxic or tense, we can feel extremes of anxiety and depression, even if things are going well in other areas of our lives. This is true of all kinds of relationships, from romantic partnerships to connections with friends and even coworkers. No matter how you know them, having good people in your life is crucial to feeling happy and whole.

If you don't believe me, take a moment to think about some of your happiest memories. Reflect for a second on the times that you felt the happiest, most hopeful, and most content. Most likely, those memories all involve at least one other person.

The Harvard study on happiness is considered one of the first psychological studies done on happiness. The study began in 1938 and tracked the lives of 741 men for 75 years. Consisting of tens of thousands of pages of research, the ultimate conclusion of this massive study was that good social relationships were *the* most important factor in living a healthy life. And though hundreds of happiness studies have been done since 1938, very few of them have yielded results that challenge this (Oppong, 2019b).

Everyone wants to be happy. However, though we often need our social connections the most when we're feeling unhappy, we tend to seek out social interaction when we're feeling happy and want to feel *happier*. When we are feeling down, our primary goal is simply to feel good in any way we can. But it's when we're feeling good that we're more likely to invest in activities that require a little more work but will bring us more benefits in the long run.

That being said, a bad relationship can be even worse for us than being alone. Chronically lonely people have been found to experience higher levels of stress and even inflammation. But people trapped in toxic relationships experience negative consequences throughout the body, including the brain.

The stress caused by not having access to a strong support system creates real, physiological damage in our brains and bodies. Lonely people have been found to have higher levels of cortisol, a stress-causing hormone, in their bloodstream. Elevated cortisol levels have been linked to a number of health challenges, including increased risk for heart disease (Oppong, 2019).

Good relationships also encourage us to behave in healthy ways. People who care about us encourage us to do things that are good for us, while toxic people encourage us to do things that might be harmful or destructive. In short, strong social connections create a continual cycle of positive emotional and physical benefits. They make us feel more secure. The people you choose to surround yourself with have a significant impact on the way you feel, behave, and see your life.

If you're a naturally social person, then it's likely none of this information comes as a surprise. But not all of us find that forming social connections comes naturally. And for some, being around other people can feel stressful or even cause anxiety. But often, the things that cause us to feel awkward, fearful, or stressed in social situations are things that come from within us, not from the people around us. And no matter how severe your social anxiety, isolating yourself from others can have devastating consequences for your physical and mental health.

Loneliness can lower your immune system function, increase anxiety, and trigger depression. Poor social connections can trigger a vicious cycle of unhappiness. Our isolation can lead to behaviors that interfere with our ability to form healthy social connections, which make us feel even more isolated. There's a reason that all of us long for close connections with friends, family, and romantic partners. Psychologically, we aren't meant to go through life alone. Our brains and bodies function much better when we're around other people (*The World Counts,* 2020).

If you're the kind of person who struggles in social situations, there are a few simple things you can try to improve the quality of your relationships with others.

Actively Make New Friends

Making new friends is a perfectly normal and acceptable goal. No one is confused about why you want to make new friends or will question why you want to expand your social circle. Force yourself to get out more. Go to events that are in line with your interests. Actively make an effort to talk to people, even if it makes you squirm on the inside (Hall, 2020). If and when you do make new friends, it will absolutely be worth it.

Make an Effort to Talk

Whether it's your barista at Starbucks, the babysitter, or your Uber driver, make an effort to talk to at least one stranger every day. One recent study found that people who made time to engage their barista in conversation enjoyed their drink more than people who didn't (Greenberg, 2015).

Turn Off Your Phone

When you're with others, at least put your phone on silent and away in your pocket. Constantly being distracted by your phone pulls you away from conversations with your roommates, partner, or children that might otherwise lead to more intimate time with them.

Ask Questions

Make conversations more personal and substantial by asking your loved ones questions about the things they care about. More importantly, make an effort to actively listen if they choose to share with you.

Reach Out

Don't wait for people to reach out to you. If you're missing someone or feeling lonely, call a friend or send someone a text. Make plans to get coffee or go for a walk.

Volunteer

There are opportunities to volunteer all around you—in your neighborhood, your child's school, or at a local non-profit. Volunteering provides you with meaningful ways to both help others in need and to connect with people who feel strongly about the same issues as you.

The benefits of social connection are almost infectious. But social connection isn't about the number of friends you have; it's about the quality of those friendships. This is how people can feel lonely or isolated in a crowd full of people or surrounded by a big family. Improving your social connections isn't necessarily about making more friends; it's about deepening connections with the friends you already have. Feeling close to the person you're talking to will enable you to trust them with your deeper thoughts and feelings. Sharing at this level is what creates truly authentic and gratifying social interactions (Hall, 2020).

Meaningful relationships support us in multiple ways and across multiple areas of our lives. According to sociologist James Michigan, a truly meaningful relationship should provide us with at least one of these kinds of support (*The World Counts*, 2020):

- Emotional - These are the people that nurture you and keep you going when times are tough. Emotional support involves love, trust, and care.
- Tangible - These are the people you can call on in times of emergency. Tangible support involves things like financial support, childcare assistance, and other material favors.
- Appraisal - In an intimate relationship, you have to trust that the feedback you're getting from the other person is honest and genuine. This type of support cannot come from casual

acquaintances. Appraisal support involves the giving of constructive and honest feedback, whether positive or negative.
- Informational - These are people like lawyers, mental health professionals, and other people who can share their expertise with you to help you. Informational support involves the sharing of relevant information and assistance in solving problems.
- Companionship - These are the kinds of people that you like to do things with. Companionship can come from clubs, religious groups, or any other social space that is centered around a specific activity.

Studies have found that healthy social connections also make us kinder and not just to our loved ones (*Do things for others,* 2020). In one famous experiment, Jonathan Stark made his Starbucks card information public and encouraged others to either use it or add money to it as they wished. As you may imagine, many people used the card, but many more people also added money to it or even left more money than they used. Scientists later explained that people were likely so generous because it felt like a social situation. Contributing money to the card made people feel like they were giving to others, and that made them feel more connected to the people who may use the card in the future, even if those people were strangers (Kogan, 2013).

Another extremely famous happiness study is the Grant study. After thousands of pages of research, the study's direction summed up its findings with one simple conclusion: "Happiness is love." (Kogan, 2013) Not wealth or power or even positive experiences. Love.

Chapter 6:

Self-Care

Keeping yourself healthy in both mind and body is crucial to your happiness and well-being. As important as it is to love and connect with others, it's equally important to foster love and care for yourself. Taking care of yourself is critical for both feelings of fulfillment and high performance in all areas of your life. And when your own needs are met, it's much easier for you to reach out and care for others. We hear it all the time on airplanes. You can't help someone with their oxygen mask until you've secured yours.

Most of us are good people. As such, we do our best to be selfless, to care for those around us, and to avoid behaving in ways that are selfish or self-serving. But viewing the world through the lens of "selfish" and "selfless" can be misleading. For example, if you wake up early in the morning to make your child a healthy breakfast, is this act selfish or selfless? You may consider it selfless because you'd really rather sleep in, but you may also consider it selfish because you love your children and the extra time you get to spend with them.

The first step in healthy self-care is distancing yourself from the concept of selfish vs. selfless. In many cases, the difference between the two is simply a matter of perspective. If you can let go of the idea that doing things for yourself is always bad, then you can release the mental blocks that are preventing you from properly taking care of yourself.

The reality is that putting yourself first is not always a bad thing. In fact, to properly and healthily care for yourself, you should be the person that you love the most. Psychologically speaking, it's impossible to love anyone else more than you love yourself. Our brains simply aren't made for it. That's why it's so difficult to feel happy when you're constantly sacrificing yourself for other people.

The key difference between healthy selflessness and unhealthy selflessness is the word "sacrifice." *Giving* is what makes you feel good, what brings you all the wonderful benefits that we talked about in chapter 5. *Sacrificing,* on the other hand, can be incredibly destructive. When our own needs aren't being met, we start to feel resentful of others when we give what little we have to them, and that can both harm our mental health and damage the quality of our relationships with others.

There's no one right or wrong way to care for yourself or others. As the circumstances of your life grow and change, so does the amount of time, energy, and money that you have to spare for others. The things that satisfy you and meet your needs in one phase of life may not be adequate in another. That's okay! As you're growing and changing, finding new purpose, new happiness, and new challenges, what your body and mind need to stay healthy will inevitably change too. This doesn't mean that life doesn't require us to make some hard choices or, yes, to make some sacrifices along the way. But the choice to sacrifice should *always* stem from feelings of meaningfulness and purpose, not from feelings of guilt or obligation (Bentley, 2018).

The Art of Self-Love

Ours is a busy and demanding world. Working, raising children, caring for elderly parents—all of these responsibilities and more can eat away at our time, money, and energy throughout the day. Self-love is the only way to balance the demands of life with the basic care that we need to stay happy and energized. Self-care is a necessary part of our wellness routine, something that we purposefully do to nourish our minds, just as we routinely eat good food or take a shower to care for our bodies. Self-care is for the self; it's something that only you can do for yourself, not something that anyone else can give you (Grey, 2017).

A few signs that you might need some self-care include (First, 2015):

- Poor sleep
- Depression and/or anxiety

- Anger and/or irritability
- High blood pressure
- Frequent illness
- Obesity
- Trouble concentrating and poor work performance
- Little or no alone time

But what does self-care mean? The true answer is anything that makes you feel relaxed, soothed, and happy. If you're not sure what that means, take a moment to reflect. Write just four or five simple activities that fill you with joy and elevate your mood. If you're still struggling for inspiration, here are a few self-care activities that can benefit anyone, no matter who you are or what your life is like (First, 2015).

Get Enough Sleep

A great deal of research has been done on sleep and the impact it has on our health and happiness. When we are sleep deprived, our stress levels increase and our risk for depression grows. And it's not just about how many hours you sleep. One study found that simply improving the *quality* of the sleep you get at night is comparable to the benefits you would get from eight weeks of therapy (Booker, 2013).

While everyone's sleep needs are different, most experts agree that the average adult needs between 7-9 hours of sleep every night. People who sleep less than seven hours a night are more likely to experience repetitive, negative thoughts throughout the day (Holmes, 2015).

If you struggle with sleep, here are a few simple tips you can try to improve the quality of your rest each night (Suni, 2021):

- Go to sleep at the same time every night, and wake up at the same time every morning.
- Don't take naps after 3 p.m.
- Don't drink caffeine or alcohol late in the day.
- Increase your exposure to bright light throughout the day.
- Reduce your screen time at night.
- Avoid nicotine entirely.
- Get regular exercise but not late at night.
- If you're hungry before bed, keep it to a light snack; don't eat a big meal right before you go to sleep.
- Make sure your bedroom is comfortable and dark.
- Do something relaxing right before you go to bed, like reading or listening to music.
- If you can't fall asleep after 20 minutes of lying in bed, don't stay there; do something calming like reading or meditating.
- Take a melatonin supplement right before bed.
- Make sure your bedroom is at a comfortable temperature.

Eat Nutritious Food

Increasingly, studies are showing that eating healthy food isn't just good for your body; it's good for your mind as well. Research shows that eating fruits and vegetables every day can increase many different factors of well-being, including happiness and general life satisfaction (Hansen, 2020). One study found that people who switched from eating almost no fruits and vegetables to eight portions of fruits and vegetables a day experienced an increase in happiness similar to the one experienced by an unemployed person finding a job (Bridges, 2019).

In fact, the impact that eating fruits and veggies has on our happiness works much faster than the positive benefits on our physical health. Eating healthy causes our brains to release a chemical called *dopamine,* which causes us to feel content and happy. And there's something to be said about the effects of being physically well on our happiness (Blaszczak-Boxe, 2016).

A diet recommended by many nutritionists for optimum happiness is the Mediterranean diet, a food plan made up primarily of fruits, vegetables, and extra-virgin olive oil. The Mediterranean diet is plant-based but not plant-exclusive like a vegetarian or vegan diet. The Mediterranean diet still includes animal products like yogurt and cheese but asks that you primarily get your protein and other macronutrients from plant-based sources like nuts and whole grains (Naidu, 2016).

Exercise

Just a little bit of physical activity can go a long way. One study found that even working out for 10 minutes a day produced a notable increase in happiness compared with people who never exercised. And the benefits of just 20 minutes of exercise can last as long as 12 hours after you've left the gym (Livingston, 2020).

Exercise makes us happy for a number of reasons (Dossantos, 2016):

- When we exercise, our heart rate increases, which in turn, increases the flow of oxygen to the brain. And as studies can prove, a well-oxygenated brain is far more resilient against anxiety and depression.
- During exercise, our brains release a number of different *endorphins,* chemicals that increase our happiness and confidence levels.
- Exercise also improves our mood simply by virtue of it being a personal growth activity; it feels good to achieve our goals, even small ones.
- Exercise grows your brain by creating new neural connections in the *hippocampus,* the region of the brain that controls memory and learning. The hippocampus is also the part of the brain that regulates our emotions.

- Exercise also improves the quality of our sleep, which means that exercising just once a day can count for two areas of self-care.

If you're struggling to find the time or the motivation to exercise regularly, here are some simple tips you can try:

- Have a fitness plan. Treat your exercise time the same way you would treat a meeting or a social engagement.
- Keep a pair of sneakers or sweatpants in your bag with you at all times.
- Exercise first thing in the morning.
- Add some extra walking into your morning commute.
- Exercise on your lunch break.
- Don't go to the gym; exercise at home.
- If your destination is within five miles, walk or bike instead of driving.

Some additional tips for maximizing your exercise plan:

- 30 minutes a day is the optimal daily workout time.
- Change the types of exercise you do; don't do the same thing every day.
- You don't have to go to the gym to exercise; walking, biking, or swimming are all excellent workouts.

- Exercise outside.
- If you can't spare a whole 30 minutes, then commit to just 10 or even five minutes a day.

Get Enough Alone Time

Though we know the benefits of being social, it's also important to get enough time for yourself. Alone time can be both restorative and replenishing, especially if we use it to indulge in activities that make us happy. Alone time gives us the privacy we need to process our strong emotions and regain a feeling of control over our lives. And the more comfortable you are being alone, the more resilience you'll have when faced with uncertain or difficult situations. Not that being alone, in and of itself, increases your resilience. Rather, alone time is when we can engage in the mental exercises that increase our resilience and mental strength. Alone time is also the time that we can spend cultivating our self-awareness, which is also necessary for full mental wellness (*Everything you need to know about happiness in one infographic,* 2020).

Paradoxically, alone time also increases our empathy and compassion for others. Solitude can increase our appreciation for the good people in our lives and enables us to return to them with renewed happiness and energy. It also increases productivity and sparks our creativity by giving us the time and space we need to think things through without distractions. In the same vein, alone time allows us to plan and reflect on our lives, giving us the time we need to make positive adjustments to our schedule or reflect on our long-term goals (Williams, n.d.).

If you have trouble feeling good when you're by yourself, here are some tips you can try:

- Simply ask yourself "What's so bad about this?"
- Schedule your alone time in a public place, like a park or a cafe.
- Commit to just five minutes a day of complete solitude, and that includes silencing your phone.
- Embrace the boredom.
- Use your alone time to go on adventures that other people might not be interested in or have time for, such as trying a new restaurant or going to a local museum.

And if you're not sure how to use your alone time in a productive way, here are some beneficial activities you can try:

- Meditation. Studies have found that people who meditate every day have increased levels of brain activity in the *prefrontal cortex,* the part of the brain that controls feelings of calm and happiness.
- Write in a journal.
- Plan and reflect on your goals.
- Process your emotions.

Indulge in your hobbies

Whether your passion is reading, yoga, or gardening, make sure that you schedule yourself time for it every day.

Committing to your self-care routine can sometimes be difficult. How often have you chosen to hit the snooze button instead of getting up and going to the gym? And if you truly need the sleep, then consider that your act of self-care for the day. But as hard as it is to wake up, you'll probably find that you feel a lot better after a day that started with exercise than after a day that started with procrastination. And the same is true for any self-care ritual. Sure, eating fast foods or sweet treats feels good. But we feel a lot better when we choose to eat foods that are healthy and nutritious. We feel good when we choose to stay home in front of Netflix or our gaming console. But we tend to feel better when we choose to go for a walk or spend some time in the garden (Kogan, 2013a).

The benefits of self-care are like the benefits of happiness itself; they are deep, subtle, and long-lasting. Self-care rituals are very small actions that have a very big effect on the quality of our lives. Remember always that self-care is never indulgent or selfish. You cannot nurture others if you aren't nurturing yourself. Take care of your own needs first, and then give to others when you find yourself with an overabundance of time, energy, or money.

Chapter 7:

Money Matters

While it's true that money can't buy happiness, it's also true that being financially unstable or unable to meet your basic needs doesn't feel good. Studies have shown that money *can* increase your sense of peace and happiness but only up to a yearly salary of $75,000. Beyond that, an increase in earnings has no substantial impact on our happiness or security. In other words, income and happiness are correlated but only up to a point. The more money we make, the less of an impact an increase in income has on our mental wellness.

So why doesn't it feel this way? How can someone who makes $80,000 or $90,000 feel stressed or struggle to pay their bills? The perception that we don't have enough money comes from what psychologists call "lifestyle creep." The more money you make, the more expensive your lifestyle becomes, and the more time you spend with people who make more money than you do. If you own a four-bedroom home, but everyone in your social circle owns a seven-bedroom mansion plus a summer home, you'll inevitably start to feel "poor" or that your income is inadequate. On a similar note, if you owned a two-bedroom home or rented a small apartment on the same income, you would probably feel like you're making a lot more money.

We mistakenly equate higher income with more happiness because we erroneously equate better or more expensive things with happiness. If you were rich, you could just buy a decadent dessert or take a bath in expensive oils when you were feeling depressed, right? If you could exercise in a beautiful gym or afford a yoga class every morning, then you'd have no problem exercising every day!

But these beliefs are erroneous. Think back to the lottery/paraplegic study. While we all love beautiful and expensive things, if you're surrounded by them all the time, they will start to lose their luster. If you purchase expensive desserts every once in a while, you'll really savor them. But if you treat yourself every time you go out, then it stops being a "treat" and becomes your everyday reality. No matter what heights of decadence we reach, we will eventually adjust to our new circumstances and return to the levels of happiness we had before we had all these fine things.

It turns out that time is more closely connected to our happiness than the number on our paychecks. If spending time with your children is something that brings you joy, you're going to start to resent a job that requires long hours or lots of travel, even if that job is paying for your children to go to college or live in a luxurious mansion. And at the end of the day, raising your children in luxury won't improve the quality of your relationship with them. In the long run, it's more beneficial for both you and your child for you to make a little less money in exchange for more free time to spend with them.

From a happiness perspective, the worst way to spend money is to purchase something that is going to cost you time as this will almost certainly add stress to your life further down the line. For example, owning a massive home with a huge lawn might seem like a step up in life, but not if it adds an extra 30 minutes to your commute or takes two hours to mow!

Have you ever wondered where the phrase "Money doesn't buy happiness" comes from? It's the conclusion of a study conducted by Richard Easterlin to investigate the impact of wealth on global happiness levels. In 1972, the nation of Bhutan made the radical political choice to focus more actively on happiness than on growing the nation's GDP. And while Bhutan continues to have a very low GDP, today it boasts one of the happiest populations on Earth, consistently ranking in happiness surveys alongside wealthier nations like Switzerland or the United States (Nelson-Coffey, 2020).

In many ways, Bhutan was ahead of its time, but the rest of the world is slowly catching up. Ruut Veenhoven is a happiness researcher with a global reputation. The World Happiness Database, something that he co-founded with other happiness researchers, continues to influence governments and organizations around the world when it comes to navigating the relationship between money and happiness. The point of the database is to make happiness research easily accessible for anyone looking to make large-scale economic changes.

In 2016, the United Nations organized a massive global survey called the "World Happiness Report." This survey ranked nations based on happiness levels according to a number of different factors to provide nations with information that could influence future policy-making. It may not surprise you that an increase in wealth had almost no bearing on the overall happiness of a nation. In fact, many of the happiest nations are some of the smallest, like Finland, Norway, and, of course, Bhutan.

Instead, scientists measure individual happiness based on three factors: the presence of positive emotions, the absence of negative emotions, and overall life satisfaction. Happiness is a purely subjective experience, meaning that no one can report on someone else's happiness; you have to ask the individual themselves. The data used by happiness reports and surveys, like the UN's, is gathered using questionnaires and other self-report measures (Nelson-Coffey, 2020).

Money vs. Happiness - How to Reconcile the Two

If you're old enough, you'll remember this Lexus advertisement from years ago. The slogan was, "Whoever said money can't buy happiness isn't spending it right." At first glance, it's easy to dismiss this advertisement as an example of the culturally endemic materialism that's causing so many of us to be miserable in the first place. But there may be more wisdom in this ad than Lexus realized or intended (Futrelle, 2017).

In recent years, more and more research has been done by economists and psychologists alike to determine the real link between money and happiness, the two forces that seem to have the most control over our daily lives. There are some essential questions about the relationship between the two that have proven relatively difficult to untangle (Kumok, 2020). Why, for example, does it seem to be the case that the more money you earn, the more money you want? Why doesn't buying a car or a home, two things that will arguably be in your life for years to come, bring you more than momentary pleasure?

So far in this book, we've explored the reasons why material things fail to bring us joy. But money buys us a lot more than fun toys or fancy upgrades. In many ways, it buys us safety, security, and autonomy. So no, buying a Lexus won't make you happy. But there is a way for all of us to have a relationship with money that does bring us lasting joy.

Research tells us that income is positively correlated with life satisfaction, but the two don't travel together in a straight line. The more money you make, the less additional happiness an increase will bring you. So the less money you make, the more of an impact an increase in income will have on your happiness. But it takes a while before an increase in pay stops increasing your happiness at all.

Just because income isn't the most important factor when it comes to measuring happiness doesn't mean that it doesn't matter at all. And the answer to true happiness isn't to forswear money altogether. If you've ever struggled to pay your rent or had your utilities shut off, you can attest to the fact that money does, to some degree, equal happiness.

Fundamentally, an increase in income doesn't make us happier, but it does make us more comfortable. Psychology distinguishes pleasure from comfort because the two are relatively different feelings. Pleasures, as we know, are fleeting. Comforts, on the other hand, are barely noticeable. Comforts improve our lives, but we don't realize just how much until we lose them.

For example, imagine you live in a place without air conditioning. When you do manage to finally install AC, life will be extremely pleasurable. But the following summer, you won't even notice the air conditioning anymore. It's gone from being a pleasure to being a comfort. As long as you have the AC unit installed, the only time you'll pay attention to it is when it breaks.

To take this a step further, a 2008 study decided to measure the brain activity in participants while they were drinking glasses of red wine. The parts of the brain that register pleasure were more active in the participants who drank wines with expensive labels than those who were drinking from bottles with $10 stickers on them. The trick? It was all the same wine; the scientists just put different labels on the different bottles. What we can learn from this study is that the quality of the wine didn't have a measurable impact on the participants' happiness. What *did* activate the brain's pleasure regions was the belief that they were drinking something expensive.

Another report (also 2008) determined that spending money on oneself had no measurable impact on happiness, but buying things for others did, indeed, seem to buy happiness. The report cited three different studies to support this conclusion. The first was an American survey that found buying gifts for people was directly correlated with an increase in personal happiness regardless of the participant's income. Incidentally, the same study found that those with a higher income level got more happiness from gift-giving than those whose income was lower.

A second company surveyed employees at a company who had all just received profit-sharing bonuses. The percentage of the bonus money each employee spent on other people directly predicted their happiness levels six to eight months later, while the percentage of the money spent on themselves seemed to not affect long-term happiness levels.

Finally, the third study was an experiment. Participants were given a $5 or a $20 and instructed either to spend the money on themselves or someone else and then their happiness levels were surveyed. The study found that regardless of the amount, those who were instructed to spend their money on someone else were significantly happier. This was despite the fact that when researchers asked participants to predict what they thought the results would be, participants reported that they believed being asked to spend $20 on yourself would yield the most happiness (Peterson, 2008).

Perhaps the most interesting thing to take from this final study is that the amount of money didn't seem to influence happiness levels at all, only the way that the money was spent. This implies that the ability to buy more expensive gifts for your loved ones won't make you any happier in the long run as long as you have the extra money to give. Remember, in the second study, people who had more money to spare got more happiness from giving to others. This is where self-care comes in. If we don't have enough money to meet our basic needs, then no amount of gift-giving or charity donations are going to bring us lasting happiness (Holder, 2017).

Money, then, is a predictor of mental wellness, but only in the sense that it protects us from stressful, negative experiences like financial insecurity and a lack of necessities. And for those who have their basic needs met, money makes us happier in the sense that it protects us from little inconveniences, like layovers or having to go grocery shopping in bad weather (Liles, 2021).

When it's used to provide for your basic needs, then it can indeed be said that money buys happiness. Access to healthcare and nutritious foods is certainly correlated with long-term life satisfaction in a very real way. According to the CDC, adults living below the poverty line are four times more likely to experience depression than adults living at or above it. The ability to meet all your basic needs while working just one job also frees up your time and energy for friends, family, and other positive social connections, which also leads to increased feelings of happiness (Entis, 2019).

Once these basic needs are met, however, Lexus is right; money can buy happiness, but it depends greatly on how you spend it. Being able to invest money in your self-care, like booking a massage or buying a new pair of shoes, can certainly contribute to your long-term happiness (Rampton, 2018). Money can be also invested in fulfilling experiences or even in improving our relationships with others. When money is used intentionally as a tool for investment in the things that are most important to us, it can greatly enhance the quality of our lives (Jewell, 2019). But when we expect that access to money or fine things is going to fulfill our deeper, emotional needs, that's when we get into trouble.

Rather than seeking to earn money for its own sake, think of money as a means you can use to achieve your long-term goals. Money in and of itself won't bring you fulfillment, so instead, think about how much money you need to make to achieve your goals (Controller, 2021). Using money to enhance and support the things that do bring you lasting happiness will transform your relationship with finances and free you from the endless striving to earn more (James, 2018).

An important perspective to cultivate is financial self-awareness. When faced with big decisions like changing jobs or working more hours, it's important to understand your current financial condition and review how making a change will affect the aspects of your life that are most important to you. Financial awareness also involves becoming more conscious of your spending. Good budgeting involves making a distinction between needs (food, housing, childcare, etc.) and wants (entertainment, restaurants, premium channels, etc.). If you're currently making enough to comfortably meet your basic needs, ask yourself honestly what a bigger salary is going to do for you. And remember, you can *always* make more money if your needs change in the future. Living within your means is an important habit to learn, one that will bring you far more financial security than any job or salary.

There's also research to suggest that spending money on experiences brings more happiness than spending money on material possessions. This is because experiences not only enhance the quality of our relationships, but they also become a positive part of our identities. Spending money on experiences that are aligned with your values can cause a significant boost in happiness. And the bonding that happens when we go on adventures or have fun experiences with others can create feelings and memories that bring us joy for years to come. Even simple activities like going to a museum or a summer day at the beach can spark deep conversations or other intimate moments with loved ones that you will treasure throughout your lifetime.

Studies also show that people tend to feel happier when they spend their money on services or goods that save them time. In one study, participants who were given $40 to spend on a time-saving service were significantly happier and less stressed at the end of the day than people who were given $40 to buy a material item. Learning to delegate our many responsibilities can prove to bring us a lot more happiness in the long run than a raise or a promotion (Mejia, 2017). Thinking about time as a finite resource can help to improve your spending choices and help you to invest more money in time-saving purchases.

And there's always the option to invest your money into things that will bring you lasting emotional benefits. If you finally manage to purchase a new home, for example, your enjoyment of it will be soured if you live with the constant fear of home invasion. In this case, investing in a home security system would be a wise investment because the emotional peace it will bring you far outweighs the cost or even the practicality of the purchase. Indulging in small, inexpensive pleasures throughout the week can also be a way to invest in your happiness. If you have the extra cash, there's no harm in treating yourself to a gourmet coffee in the morning, especially if you enjoy it and it brightens your day.

Chapter 8:

The Meaning of Life

Last but certainly not least, finding your life's purpose or working toward important, long-term goals is a key component of living a happy life. Feeling connected to a deeper purpose or mission gives you a meaningful structure around which to organize your life. Studies show that people who have more meaning in their lives experience more stable moods and demonstrate more prosocial behaviors. This is true across multiple ages, backgrounds, and nationalities.

People find meaning in multiple different areas of life, including:

- A fulfilling career
- Spirituality or religion
- Raising children
- Pursuing goals that align with their core values

Goals that include a commitment to others, including family, friends, or a greater community, have been found to provide more overall life satisfaction than goals that only benefit ourselves. Spiritual practices, like meditation or prayer, have been found to increase brain activity in the prefrontal cortex, the area of the brain responsible for feelings of happiness and a sense of calm. And doing things that benefit others increases our capacity for empathy. This, in turn, increases our intimacy with others, improving the quality of our relationships and bringing us happiness.

Science tells us that who people feel like they have a purpose in life have better mental wellness and feel more fulfilled. When we talk about having a purpose, we mean people who have clear, long-term goals who feel like they have direction in life. Having a sense of purpose is something that happens naturally for some but is something that you can actively cultivate if it doesn't come naturally to you. Finding life's purpose essentially involves two steps: finding a goal that you care deeply about and taking productive steps that will get you closer to achieving that goal (*Everything you need to know about happiness in one infographic*, 2020).

Life purposes are big-picture. Achieving them means contributing to the well-being of all humanity, and knowing this inevitably makes us feel good. In addition, having big life goals has been linked to a number of benefits. These include (Cherry, 2020):

- Increased life satisfaction
- Better coping skills
- Better physical health. Some studies have even found that people who have meaning in their lives tend to live longer.
- Better resilience. Resilience is one of our happy habits, and it turns out that it's much easier to

build if you feel that your life has meaning. One study found that people whose lives have purpose tend to have lower levels of cortisol, a stress-causing hormone, in their bloodstreams.

- People with meaningful lives find it easier to engage in self-care activities, such as eating healthy or engaging in daily exercise.
- People with meaningful lives also tend to get sick less often. One study found that having a sense of purpose was linked to improved immune function.

Having a sense of purpose directly and indirectly increases your happiness levels. Meaning doesn't just make you happy in and of itself; it also makes you more likely to engage in other activities, like self-care or giving to others, that naturally bring happiness as well. Those who have meaningful lives, for example, find it easier to make time for self-care than those who don't. This is because people with a purpose have a clearer idea of how to structure their lives, where to invest their money, and how to best spend their time than those who are unsure of what they want to achieve in life.

And self-care isn't the only road to happiness that having a life purpose may open. Those who have a sense of purpose in their lives also tend to be more grateful than those who don't. Those who have a sense of purpose are more likely to both notice and appreciate when they get a lucky break than those who don't. And the increased gratitude practices on the part of those who have a distinct life purpose inevitably bring them more happiness than people who feel more aimless.

Having a purpose, it seems, puts you on the fast-track to happiness. Like money, having a purpose in and of itself doesn't necessarily equal happiness. But unlike money, having a sense of purpose seems to instigate happiness-inducing behaviors and makes it easier to commit to habits that will bring us more happiness in the long term.

Simply having a sense of purpose makes you feel more fulfilled, even if you do nothing to achieve it. Having a sense of purpose means having clear life goals and feeling that achieving those life goals is important for yourself and others. It's this deep-seated belief that achieving your goals is universally important that makes you more willing to engage in healthy and happy habits.

If you're struggling to find a sense of purpose in your own life, there are a few things you can do, including (Cherry, 2020):

- Explore your interests and passions.
- Engage in prosocial and altruistic activities.
- Work to address and educate others on social injustices.
- Look for new things you want to learn about.

Remember, a sense of purpose is something that can either happen to you naturally or you can actively work to cultivate. If you discover something that you care deeply about, you will inevitably engage in positive actions that will take you closer to achieving that goal. Even if you don't have a specific goal in mind, simply finding something that you're deeply passionate about can give your life some kind of structure and guide you toward specific actions that will leave you feeling more deeply fulfilled.

Finding Your Life's Purpose

If you're not sure what your life's purpose is, then you're in good company. Fortunately, it's often the pursuit of a life's purpose that puts us on the path to happiness.

To get you started, try this simple visualization. Imagine what your life would be like years into the future if everything went your way (Vacik, 2021). If you had everything you've ever wanted and achieved everything you've ever wanted to achieve, what would that look like? How would you live? Who would you live with? What would daily reality look like in your perfect reality?

When you visualize, be as specific as possible. If your ideal reality involves a job, for example, examine exactly what you would do and who you would be working with. The clearer your vision is, the easier it will be to set achievable goals that will bring you ever closer to your ideal vision (Nikutowski, 2021).

What do you want people to say at your funeral? Make a list of things that you want people to remember about you long after you're dead and consider that your long-term to-do list. True happiness requires a balance between self-love and forging strong social connections. Purpose is what helps us to navigate this balance. Meaningful actions are the ones that you do for yourself but ultimately bring you joy because of the positive effects they have on the world around you. Whether your life's goal is to be a great writer, start your own business, or be an amazing father, you first embark on these life paths because these things bring *you* joy. But all of these roles and more can contribute a great deal of positivity to the world. As you pursue your life's purpose, seeing how pursuing your goals benefits other people can fill you with deep feelings of pride and lasting joy.

Often, our purpose in life is already embedded in our daily joys. It's not a matter of "finding" it as much as it is a matter of noticing it. Having clear life goals is what gives us hope and the ability to imagine a better future for ourselves. The successful pursuit of meaningful goals has incredible psychological benefits, including (*5 Reasons having goals can make you happier,* 2020):

- Giving us hope and something to look forward to in life
- Increasing our sense of meaning and purpose
- Increasing our motivation levels

- Helping us to map out exactly what it is we want to achieve in life
- Helping us grow into the best possible version of ourselves
- Giving us a clear source of interest and engagement
- Focusing our attention
- Bringing us a sense of achievement and confidence when we achieve what we set out to do
- Bringing us a sense of happiness and satisfaction when we move visibly closer to our goals. And increased happiness, in turn, motivates us to work even harder to achieve our goals, creating a beneficial cycle of motivation and achievement.

Without goals, we tend to wander through life wondering why nothing is changing instead of actively working to learn and improve ourselves. Without purpose, we tend to succumb to self-pity and the toxic mindset of a victim mentality. Purpose gives us the motivation that we need to actively change our lives and the power to take responsibility for our fate. Without clear goals to work toward, we start to feel more and more powerless to change our lives.

If you find yourself constantly thinking "I wish…" or "If only…," then it may be time to sit down and rethink your life goals. When we have no clear goals, we tend to see the world as a hostile place, making generalizing statements like "Everyone hates me" or "No one supports me." But when we have a purpose in life, we realize quickly that these generalizing statements aren't true. When we have something specific to work toward, it's also easier for us to see the specific obstacles that are standing in our path. When your life has meaning, "everyone" can be reduced to "my mom" or "my boss," and then you can take steps to remedy the negative situation to move closer to your ultimate life goals.

The best goals are ones that are challenging yet still attainable. Challenging enough to excite and interest us but still realistic enough for us to achieve them. No one can tell you what your goals are or should be; they can only be meaningful if they are driven by your personal values. Choose goals that will make you happy in the long run rather than trying to pursue external markers of success like fame or wealth. Intrinsic goals will be much more satisfying to both pursue and achieve because they satisfy our core psychological needs for autonomy, relatedness, and competence. When choosing goals for yourself, choose things that will satisfy your own psychological needs, things that aren't reliant on the judgment or approval of others (*Have goals for the future*, 2020).

Big life goals don't have to be long-term either. Anything that brings you closer to your ideal version of reality is a life goal and worth pursuing. A metric for goal setting that has become popular in the business world is SMART, or specific, measurable, action-oriented, reasonable, and time-oriented (Sokol, 2020).

Once you know what your goals are, it can also be helpful to create an action plan, one that outlines clearly the steps you need to take to achieve them. Creating an action plan helps us to keep our long-term goals in sight while we focus on all of the little goals we need to conquer to achieve them. For example, if one of your goals is to climb Mt. Everest, then your action plan will include all the things you would need to do to prepare for such a venture, like strength training, a list of smaller mountains to hike first, and a list of all the gear you need to buy (Brolley, 2019).

To create an action plan, there are a few simple steps you can follow:

- Create goals specific to each of the primary roles in your life.
- Remember that it's always possible to change and improve; there's no such thing as a "mistake-proof" goal.
- Once you've identified your big life goals, break them down into smaller, short-term targets.

When thinking about your goals, ask yourself the following questions:

- What are my core values?
- What do I want to achieve in my lifetime?

- Who am I, and how will achieving my goals define my identity?
- Do I already have a mission in life?
- If so, what is it?
- What would I do to defend the things I believe in?

Without an action plan, it's all too easy to sabotage yourself by biting off more than you can chew and getting discouraged because of it. If you want to become an Olympic athlete, you're probably not ready for the tryouts just yet. If you want to start your own business, you should probably do some research or lay out a business plan before you apply for a business loan. Without an action plan, we sometimes get too excited and try to take on more than we're ready for. And when our grand plans inevitably fall through, we blame ourselves or decide that maybe our goals aren't achievable after all. Creating an action plan will help you to pursue your goal in small, achievable steps so that you can slowly but surely work your way up to fulfilling any dream you put your mind to (Pychyl, 2008).

Of course, things can go awry in your action plan as well, but having the plan will make it easier for you to regroup and learn from your mistakes rather than letting them discourage you or cause you to give up on your goals entirely.

Conclusion

What you have in your hands is a roadmap to happiness. By following the eight methods outlined in this book, you will find your life transformed by the good feelings and positivity that come your way.

Now that you've read through the book, you can choose to use it in one of two ways. I would recommend working through the book chapter by chapter. Begin by recognizing and letting go of some of your toxic habits, as outlined in chapter 1. From there, progress to chapter 2, where you can start to think about what happiness means to you, then to chapter 3, and so on. I've outlined the book in this way so that you can follow its guidance step by step. Once you feel like you've mastered one step, you can move on to the next chapter and try making those new changes to your life.

However, you can also feel free to jump around. If there was a chapter or a section that really spoke deeply to you, start there! Only you know what's going on inside you, and only you know what you really need to do to make a lasting change in your life.

My mission for this book is to give you one tiny feeling that we haven't talked about yet: hope. Too many people get stuck in feelings of depression, despair, and cynicism because they believe there's nothing they can do to change their lives. While reading this book, even if you chose to begin from the very beginning, my sincere hope is that you realized just how many options you have available to you. No one's life is fixed or unchangeable. You may have huge obstacles standing in the way of your happiness, or you may need a few simple, daily adjustments. Either way, you *do* have the power to live the life of your dreams. At the very least, you have the power to live a life that you like.

Not every exercise in this book will work for you, and that's okay. Everyone's needs, lives, and lifepaths are slightly different. If something isn't working for you, feel free to skip over it. But no matter who you are or what your life is like, there's something in this book for everything. The guidance in this book has been compiled from hundreds of different articles and studies, but it's also come from my own lived experiences. These eight paths to happiness are ones that I had to learn the hard way. With this book in your hand, you can skip all of the pain and confusion that I once experienced.

So with that being said, don't wait to try some of the changes outlined in this book. Even if you try just one simple thought exercise or spend some time thinking over just one paragraph that spoke to you, you'll already begin to notice the change within yourself. Life is far too short to spend it being miserable. You have all the tools you need; it's time to go out and use them!

If you enjoyed this book, I'd love to hear your feedback, and I know others could benefit from it too! Don't forget to leave a review on Amazon so that other people can join you on your journey toward a brighter future.

References

5 Reasons Having Goals Can Make You Happier. (2020, November 4). Proud Happy Brave. https://proud-happy-brave.com/having-goals-can-make-you-happier/

10 Ways Sleep Makes Us Healthier, Happier and More Successful. (2019, July 26). Canyon Ranch. https://www.canyonranch.com/blog/health/10-ways-sleep-makes-us-healthier-happier-and-more-successful/

Ackerman, C. M. E. (2020, October 31). *What Is Happiness and Why Is It Important?* PositivePsychology.Com. https://positivepsychology.com/what-is-happiness/

Adventskalender 2020 | RITUALS | Exclusieve Kerstkalender. (2020). Rituals. https://www.rituals.com/nl-nl/adventskalender.html

Babauta, L. (2012, September 26). *How to Find Happiness Within.* Zen Habits. https://zenhabits.net/happiness-within/

Baltazzi, M. (2019, August 2). *Why Science Says Helping Others Makes Us Happier.* Thriveglobal.Com. https://thriveglobal.com/stories/why-science-says-helping-others-makes-us-happier/

Bathla, S. (2020, December 11). *5 Reasons Why Most People Are Not Happy & How to Resolve Them!* Medium. https://medium.com/multiplier-magazine/5-reasons-why-most-people-are-not-happy-how-to-resolve-this-b8d73d9e080c

Becker, J. (2020). *Nine Reasons Buying Stuff Will Never Make You Happy.* Becomingminimalist.Com. https://www.becomingminimalist.com/buying-stuff-wont-make-you-happy/

Belli, G. (2017, September 13). *7 Tips For Staying Passionate About Your Work.* PayScale. https://www.payscale.com/career-news/2017/09/7-tips-staying-passionate-work

Bentley, L. (2018, August 24). *Why putting yourself first improves your happiness and productivity.* NBC News. https://www.nbcnews.com/know-your-value/feature/why-putting-yourself-first-improves-your-happiness-productivity-ncna903216

Bjergegaard, M. (2014, April 28). *How to Fit Exercise into Your Routine—No Matter How Busy You Are.*

Greatist. https://greatist.com/fitness/how-to-fit-exercise-into-a-busy-work-schedule#1

Blaszczak-Boxe, A. (2016, July 14). *Eating More Fruits & Veggies May Make You Happier*. Livescience.Com. https://www.livescience.com/55407-eating-more-fruits-veggies-linked-with-life-satisfaction.html

Booker, K. (2013). *Good night's sleep linked to happiness.* Cornell Chronicle. https://news.cornell.edu/stories/2013/04/good-nights-sleep-linked-happiness

Bradberry, T. (2016, November 3). *12 Reasons You're Not As Happy As You Should Be*. Forbes. https://www.forbes.com/sites/travisbradberry/2016/10/25/12-reasons-youre-not-as-happy-as-you-should-be/?sh=5e0627a51dd0

Brech, A. (2020, April 27). *Why spending time alone makes us happy.* Flash Pack. https://www.flashpack.com/wellness/spending-time-alone/

Bridges, F. (2019, February 25). *Healthy Food Makes You Happy: Research Shows A Healthy Diet Improves Your Mental Health*. Forbes. https://www.forbes.com/sites/francesbridges/2019/01/26/food-makes-you-happy-a-healthy-diet-improves-mental-health/?sh=745b3fad26f8

Brolley, B. (2019, July 25). *The Real Reasons You're Not Happy*. TheList.Com. https://www.thelist.com/159867/the-real-reasons-youre-not-happy/

Cabelly, H. (2016, July 26). *How to Rise Above Difficult Circumstances and Be Happy*. Tiny Buddha. https://tinybuddha.com/blog/how-to-rise-difficult-circumstances-be-happy/

Cherry, K. (2020). *How Do Psychologists Define Happiness?* Verywell Mind. https://www.verywellmind.com/what-is-happiness-4869755

Christian, C. (2020, December 13). *Causes Of Unhappiness: Why Everyone Is So Unhappy (With Examples)*. Tracking Happiness. https://www.trackinghappiness.com/causes-of-unhappiness/

Controller, C. (2021, January 21). *3 Ways to Change Your Perspective about Money*. Complete Controller. https://www.completecontroller.com/3-ways-to-change-your-perspective-about-money/

Cudmore, D. (2019). *How a Hobby Can Make You Live a Happier Life*. Thriveglobal.Com. https://thriveglobal.com/stories/how-a-hobby-can-make-you-live-a-happier-life/

Davis, T. (2018). *Thirty-Nine Core Values and How to Live Them*. Psychologytoday.Com. https://www.psychologytoday.com/us/blog/click-here-happiness/201807/39-core-values-and-how-live-them

Dee, K. (2011, August 8). *5 Scientific Reasons Your Idea of Happiness Is Wrong*. Cracked.Com. https://www.cracked.com/article_19376_5-scientific-reasons-your-idea-happiness-wrong.html

DiGiulio, S. (2018, January 9). *In good company: Why we need other people to be happy*. NBC News. https://www.nbcnews.com/better/health/good-company-why-we-need-other-people-be-happy-ncna836106

Do things for others. (2020). Action for Happiness. https://www.actionforhappiness.org/10-keys-to-happier-living/do-things-for-others/details

Dossantos, N. (2016, February 5). *8 Ways to Exercise on a Busy Schedule*. The Active Times. https://www.theactivetimes.com/fitness/your-first-time/8-ways-exercise-busy-schedule

Entis, L. (2019, November 20). *Can money buy happiness? It sure can*. Vox. https://www.vox.com/the-highlight/2019/11/13/20951937/money-experiences-buy-happiness-happy-how-to-spend

Everything You Need to Know About Happiness in One Infographic. (n.d.). Happify.Com. https://www.happify.com/hd/science-of-happiness-infographic/

Farewell, A. (2016, June 24). *Self-Acceptance: The Key To True Happiness.* Dumb Little Man. https://www.dumblittleman.com/how-to-accept-yourself/

Find a Passion That Makes You Happy. (2016, November 1). Happiness Matters. https://happinessmatters.com/passion-that-makes-you-happy/

Finding Your Passion is One Major Key in Happiness. (2021). UniversalClass.Com. https://www.universalclass.com/articles/self-help/finding-your-passion-is-one-major-key-in-happiness.htm

Fink, J. (2020, December 16). *6 Ways to Build a Healthy Relationship With Money.* The Dollar Stretcher. https://www.thedollarstretcher.com/personal-finance/ways-to-build-a-healthy-relationship-with-money/

First, Y. (2015). *Self Care Leads to Happiness.* Youfirstinc.Org. https://youthfirstinc.org/self-care-leads-to-happiness/

Futrelle, D. (2017, August 7). *Here's How Money Really Can Buy You Happiness.* Time. https://time.com/4856954/can-money-buy-you-happiness/

Goldsmith, B. (2012). *Ten Simple Ways to Find Happiness.* Psychologytoday.Com. https://www.psychologytoday.com/us/blog/emotional-fitness/201204/10-simple-ways-find-happiness

Gratitude and Happiness. (2020, July 19). Psychological & Counseling Services. https://www.unh.edu/pacs/gratitude-happiness

Greenberg, M. (2015). *How Gratitude Leads to a Happier Life.* Psychologytoday.Com. https://www.psychologytoday.com/us/blog/the-mindful-self-express/201511/how-gratitude-leads-happier-life

Grey, S. (2017, June 19). *Self-Care and Happiness: When You're Right Your World is Right.* Esteemology. https://esteemology.com/self-care-and-happiness-when-youre-right-your-world-is-right/

Hall, K. (2020). *Happiness Is About Connecting.* Psychologytoday.Com. https://www.psychologytoday.com/us/blog/pieces-mind/202008/happiness-is-about-connecting

Hansen, P. (2020). *How Eating Healthy Can Make Us Happy.* Feast. https://vocal.media/feast/how-eating-healthy-can-make-us-happy

happiness.com. (2020, December 18). *12 ways to practise self-acceptance.* https://www.happiness.com/magazine/personal-growth/self-acceptance/

Harvard Health Publishing. (2011). *Giving thanks can make you happier.* Harvard Health. https://www.health.harvard.edu/healthbeat/giving-thanks-can-make-you-happier

Have goals for the future. (2020). Action for Happiness. https://www.actionforhappiness.org/10-keys-to-happier-living/have-goals-to-look-forward-to/details

Holder, M. (2017). *Three Ways Money Buys Happiness.* Psychologytoday.Com. https://www.psychologytoday.com/intl/blog/the-happiness-doctor/201708/three-ways-money-buys-happiness

Holmes, L. (2015). *All the Ways Sleep Affects Your Happiness in One Post*. Huffpost.Com. https://www.huffpost.com/entry/all-the-ways-sleep-affects-your-happiness-in-one-char_n_55ae4d55e4b07af29d564a29

Iliff, R. (2015, June 9). *7 Tips for Loving Your Career and Working With Passion*. Entrepreneur. https://www.entrepreneur.com/article/247017

INFOGRAPHIC: Here's Why Exercise Really Makes You Happier. (2020). Happify.Com. https://my.happify.com/hd/exercise-and-happiness-infographic/

INFOGRAPHIC: How Our Hobbies Make Us Happier. (2020). Happify.Com. https://www.happify.com/hd/how-our-hobbies-make-us-happier/

Itani, O. (2020, January 29). *Solitude: The Importance and Benefits of Spending Time Alone*. OMAR ITANI. https://www.omaritani.com/blog/spending-time-alone

James, J. (2018, September 14). *Money is a Means, not an End*. Life In Charge. https://lifeincharge.com/money-is-a-means-not-an-end/

Jewell, T. (2019, October 29). *Can You Buy Happiness?* Healthline. https://www.healthline.com/health/can-money-buy-happiness

Jones, E. (2009, February 17). *5 Things You Think Will Make You Happy (But Won't)*. Cracked.Com. https://www.cracked.com/article_17061_reminder-5-things-you-think-will-make-you-happy-but-wont.html

Kogan, N. (2013a). *Self-care isn't an extra. It's your fuel. - Happier.* Happier.Com. https://www.happier.com/blog/self-care-isnt-extra-its-your-fuel/

Kogan, N. (2013b). *The magic of a good night's sleep - Happier.* Happier.Com. https://www.happier.com/blog/the-magic-of-sleep/

Kogan, N. (2013c). *The single most important thing we can do for our happiness - Happier.* Happier.Com. https://www.happier.com/blog/how-to-find-happiness-the-single-most-important-thing-we-can-do/

Kumok, Z. (2020, January 23). *4 times money can actually buy you happiness, according to research*. Business Insider. https://www.businessinsider.com/personal-finance/money-can-actually-buy-you-happiness-according-to-research?international=true&r=US&IR=T

Lemmetty, H. (2019, June 19). *9 Ways To Make Time For Exercise With A Busy Schedule*. Polar Blog. https://www.polar.com/blog/9-ways-how-to-make-time-for-exercise/

Life, V. (2018, August 13). *How Hobbies Make You Happier And Healthier*. Life & Health Network. https://lifeandhealth.org/lifestyle/how-hobbies-make-you-happier-and-healthier/1411136.html

Liles, H. (2021, January 6). *Money can buy happiness: Here's how much you need and how to spend it, according to a financial therapist*. Insider. https://www.insider.com/can-money-buy-happiness

Livingston, M. (2020, February 12). *4 ways exercise can make you happier -- even if you don't like to exercise*. CNET. https://www.cnet.com/health/ways-exercise-makes-you-happier/

Local community. (2020). Action for Happiness. https://www.actionforhappiness.org/10-keys-to-happier-living/local-community/details

Lyubomirsky, S. (n.d.). *3 Myths of Happiness Everyone Should Stop Believing*. Happify.Com. https://www.happify.com/hd/3-myths-of-happiness/

Lyubomirsky, S. (2017, November 1). *Eight Ways Gratitude Boosts Happiness*. Gratefulness.Org. https://gratefulness.org/resource/eight-ways/

M, K. (2018, November 16). *5 Easy Ways to Feed Your Soul and Add (More) Happiness to Your Life*. Medium. https://medium.com/@kalleenmarq/5-easy-ways-to-feed-your-soul-and-add-more-happiness-to-your-life-5d4b0fa368d9

Markman, A. (2018, November 2). *Secrets of people who stay happy in the worst circumstances*. Fast Company. https://www.fastcompany.com/90253795/secrets-of-people-who-stay-happy-in-the-worst-circumstances

Martin, K. (2019, September 10). *How to Think Like an Optimist*. Goop. https://goop.com/wellness/mindfulness/how-to-think-like-an-optimist/

Mawer, R. (2020). *Seventeen Proven Tips to Sleep Better at Night*. Healthline.Com. https://www.healthline.com/nutrition/17-tips-to-sleep-better

Mejia, Z. (2017, November 10). *A psychology expert says spending your money on this can boost your happiness.* CNBC. https://www.cnbc.com/2017/11/10/psychology-expert-says-spending-your-money-on-this-can-boost-happiness.html

mindbodygreen. (2020, June 17). *6 Reasons Exercise Makes You Happy.* https://www.mindbodygreen.com/0-10798/6-reasons-why-exercise-makes-you-happy.html

Monster. (n.d.). *6 ways to reignite your passion for work.* Monster Career Advice. https://www.monster.com/career-advice/article/6-ways-to-reignite-your-passion-for-work-1117

Morin, A. (2017, August 7). *7 Science-Backed Reasons You Should Spend More Time Alone.* Forbes. https://www.forbes.com/sites/amymorin/2017/08/05/7-science-backed-reasons-you-should-spend-more-time-alone/?sh=2dbdf6671b7e

Morin, A. (2020). *How to Be Optimistic When Everyone Else Isn't.* Verywell Mind. https://www.verywellmind.com/how-to-be-optimistic-4164832

Naidu, D. (2016, July 18). *How Eating Healthy Can Make You Happy -.* Skilledatlife.Com.

http://www.skilledatlife.com/how-eating-healthy-can-make-you-happy/

Neilson, S. (2018, January 8). *Why Hobbies Make You Happy*. The Cut. https://www.thecut.com/2018/01/why-hobbies-make-you-happy.html

Nelson-Coffey, K. (2020, September 1). *The Science of Happiness in Positive Psychology 101*. PositivePsychology.Com. https://positivepsychology.com/happiness/

Newsonen, S. (2014). *Can You Find Happiness Through Passion?* Psychologytoday.Com. https://www.psychologytoday.com/us/blog/the-path-passionate-happiness/201404/can-you-find-happiness-through-passion

Nikutowski, N. (2021, January 5). *How Working on Your Goals Makes you Happy*. Happiness On. https://happinesson.com/how-working-on-your-goals-makes-you-happy/

Nyx, J. (2020, January 2). *How to Be Happy in Life (Despite Your Circumstances)*. Lifehack. https://www.lifehack.org/859328/how-to-be-happy-in-life

Oppong, T. (2019a). *Good Social Relationships Are The Most Consistent Predictor of a Happy Life*. Thriveglobal.Com.
https://thriveglobal.com/stories/relationships-happiness-well-being-life-lessons/

Oppong, T. (2019b, October 18). *Good Social Relationships Are The Most Consistent Predictor of a Happy Life*. Medium.
https://medium.com/kaizen-habits/good-social-relationships-are-the-strongest-most-consistent-predictor-of-a-happy-life-742d234cc5d2

Orsini, M. (2019). *We've Got Happiness ALL WRONG!* Thriveglobal.Com.
https://thriveglobal.com/stories/weve-got-happiness-all-wrong/

Parks, A. (2021). *What Is Happiness, Anyway?* Happify.Com.
https://www.happify.com/hd/what-is-happiness-anyway/

Peterson, C. (2008). *Money and Happiness*. Psychologytoday.Com.
https://www.psychologytoday.com/us/blog/the-good-life/200806/money-and-happiness

Pomeroy, R. (2014). *The Things We Think Make Us Happy… Don't | RealClearScience*.

Realclearscience.Com.
https://www.realclearscience.com/blog/2014/07/the_things_we_think_make_us_happy_dont.html

Positive Thinking: Optimism, Gratitude and Happiness. (2017, September 6). Pursuit of Happiness.
https://www.pursuit-of-happiness.org/science-of-happiness/positive-thinking/

Pychyl, T. (2008). *Goal Progress and Happiness.* Psychologytoday.Com.
https://www.psychologytoday.com/us/blog/dont-delay/200806/goal-progress-and-happiness#

Rampton, J. (2018, March 2). *Science Says Money Does Buy Happiness If You Spend It the Right Way.* Entrepreneur.
https://www.entrepreneur.com/article/309814

Robinson, B. (2019, November 18). *The Power Of Gratitude And How It Raises Your Happiness Level.* Forbes.
https://www.forbes.com/sites/bryanrobinson/2019/11/18/the-power-of-gratitude-and-how-it-raises-your-happiness-level/?sh=1c2f0d1f373e

Rubin, G. (2017, October 21). *Why PASSION is so critically important to happiness.* Gretchen Rubin.

https://gretchenrubin.com/2007/04/why_passion_is_/

Sandoiu, A. (2017, March 20). *Better sleep can make us feel like a million bucks.* Medicalnewstoday.Com. https://www.medicalnewstoday.com/articles/316445

Santi, J. (n.d.). *The Secret to Happiness is Helping Others.* Time.Com. https://time.com/collection/guide-to-happiness/4070299/secret-to-happiness/

Schumer, L. (2018, October 11). *Why Following Your Passions Is Good for You (and How to Get Started).* The New York Times. https://www.nytimes.com/2018/10/10/smarter-living/follow-your-passion-hobbies-jobs-self-care.html

Scott, S. (2020, June 11). *How Optimism Affects Your Happiness.* Happier Human. https://www.happierhuman.com/optimism-happiness/

Seltzer, L. (2008). *The Path to Unconditional Self-Acceptance.* Psychologytoday.Com. https://www.psychologytoday.com/intl/blog/evolution-the-self/200809/the-path-unconditional-self-acceptance

Simon, S. (2020, May 5). *10 Tips to Get More Sleep.* Cancer.Org. https://www.cancer.org/latest-news/how-to-get-more-sleep.html

Singh, S. (2019, May 18). *How Optimism Affects Happiness.* Love Equals. https://loveequals.net/blogs/sports/how-optimism-affects-happiness

Sokol, J. (2020, June 19). *20 Tips: How to Set Goals That Actually Make You Happy :).* Sensophy. https://www.sensophy.com/how-to-set-goals-that-actually-make-you-happy/

Steber, C. (2016, September 2). *11 Tips For Spending Time Alone & Actually Enjoying It.* Bustle. https://www.bustle.com/articles/181665-11-tips-for-spending-time-alone-actually-enjoying-it

Steinhilber, B. (2017, August 24). *How to Train Your Brain to Be More Optimistic.* NBC News. https://www.nbcnews.com/better/health/how-train-your-brain-be-more-optimistic-ncna795231

Stoerkel, E. M. (2020, December 4). *The Science and Research on Gratitude and Happiness.* PositivePsychology.Com. https://positivepsychology.com/gratitude-happiness-research/

Suni, E. (2021, January 9). *How to Sleep Better*. Sleep Foundation. https://www.sleepfoundation.org/sleep-hygiene/healthy-sleep-tips

Tan, A. (2017, May 27). *7 Wrong Ideas About Happiness You Need to Eliminate*. Pick the Brain | Motivation and Self Improvement. https://www.pickthebrain.com/7-wrong-ideas-about-happiness-you-need-to-eliminate/

Team, R. (2019, April 16). *How To Fit Exercise Into Your Busy Life*. Realbuzz 5. https://www.realbuzz.com/articles-interests/fitness/article/how-to-fit-exercise-into-your-busy-life/

Tejvan, T. (2008, April 16). *The Difference between False Happiness and Real Happiness – Happiness will follow you*. Srichinmoybio.Co.Uk. https://www.srichinmoybio.co.uk/blog/happiness/the-difference-between-false-happiness-and-real-happiness/

The World Counts. (2020). Theworldcounts.Com. https://www.theworldcounts.com/happiness/social-connections-and-happiness

Tim, T. (2018, August 10). *8 Causes of Modern Unhappiness - Mission.org*. Medium.

https://medium.com/the-mission/8-causes-of-modern-unhappiness-a78164dd1ec0

University of Hertfordshire (2014, March 7). *Self-acceptance could be the key to a happier life, yet it's the happy habit many people practice the least.* ScienceDaily. https://www.sciencedaily.com/releases/2014/03/140307111016.htm

Vacik, C. (2021, January 19). *How to Set Life Goals That Ensure Success and Happiness.* Lifehack. https://www.lifehack.org/444514/how-to-set-life-goals-that-ensure-success-and-happiness

Vozza, S. (2018, November 21). *This is what you're getting wrong about your pursuit of happiness.* Fast Company. https://www.fastcompany.com/90266718/what-youre-getting-wrong-about-your-pursuit-of-happiness

White, R., & White, R. (2014). *https://www.connectinghappinessandsuccess.com/blogs/*. Connectinghappinessandsuccess.Com. https://www.connectinghappinessandsuccess.com/how-optimism-can-help-you-be-happier/

Williams, L. (n.d.). *The Key to Happiness: Spending Time Alone.* Readersdigest.Co.Uk.

https://www.readersdigest.co.uk/health/wellbeing/the-key-to-happiness-spending-time-alone

Wingman Magazine. (2020, August 11). *8 Reasons Why Getting Involved in Your Community Can Make You Happier (and How to Start)*. Wingman Magazine - The "Dark Web" of Personal Development. https://get-a-wingman.com/8-reasons-why-getting-involved-in-your-community-can-make-you-happier-and-how-to-start/

Wojno, R. (n.d.). *6 Reasons Why Having Some Alone Time Is Really Good for You*. Happify.Com. https://my.happify.com/hd/why-having-alone-time-is-good-for-you/

Wolff, C. (2018, April 12). *Shockingly, These 7 Things Don't Actually Make You Happy, According To Science*. Bustle. https://www.bustle.com/p/shockingly-these-7-things-dont-actually-make-you-happy-according-to-science-8753299

www.ingramcontent.com/pod-product-compliance
Lightning Source LLC
Chambersburg PA
CBHW050318120526
44592CB00014B/1963